Praise for *Covert Cows and Chick-fil-A*

"The Cow campaign became an endearing part of American pop culture largely because of an independent, family-owned business armed with conviction. . . . The successful launch of the Eat Mor Chikin movement required great courage from a CMO who saw an original idea and approved it based on his instincts."

Stan Richards, founder and creative director, The Richards Group

"This is a must-read for anyone who dares to dream big, is seeking purpose in their lives, has ambition, or wants a formula for business and life success."

Scott Davis, chief growth officer, Prophet

"This book is an excellent 'backstage tour' of Chick-fil-A from its prebrand days to how it became a nationally respected brand."

Gene Ontjes, Chick-fil-A Operator

"*Covert Cows and Chick-fil-A* could be assigned as supplemental reading for a graduate-level class in marketing . . . I also see this as a book that should be on the list of recommended readings for all undergraduate business students."

Bill C. Hardgrave, provost, Auburn University

"Steve Robinson used simple ingredients to create his successful marketing recipe for Chick-fil-A: a chicken sandwich, uneducated cows, and enlightened customers. In this book the genius himself reveals how he did it."

Jimmy Collins, former president amd chief operating officer of Chick-fil-A

"Steve captures the very essence of the Chick-fil-A culture and the legacy of our founder, S. Truett Cathy. This book should be required reading for all new Chick-fil-A Operators and it certainly will help any business person who wants to take their brand to a higher level."

Nelson Pete Burgess, Chick-fil-A Operator

"You will enjoy reading this fantastic inside look at how and why Chick-fil-A grew from an idea into a national brand. Steve's book outlines the foundation that this amazing company is based on: faith, family, loyalty, and lots of hard work."

Phillip Fulmer, athletic director at
the University of Tennessee

"Steve's brand-building story is now required reading for my Northwestern University Medill IMC students and one I highly recommend for anyone who wants to better understand the extraordinary power of a higher-purpose-driven brand, a strong culture, clear and meaningful goals, and insightful strategies and execution."

Marty Kohr, faculty, Northwestern University Medill IMC

"If you are looking for a *great* read that is loaded with life lessons, wisdom, and values that will impact your life . . . *you've found it!* Steve does a fabulous job of telling the remarkable and compelling story of Chick-fil-A's success and Truett Cathy's model of purposeful leadership. *Covert Cows and Chick-fil-A* isn't just entertaining; it will equip you to be a missional leader at work, at home, and in your community."

Dr. Dennis Rainey, cofounder of FamilyLife

"*Covert Cows* is a stellar, inspiring read for anyone wanting to embrace wisdom and foster innovation in the marketplace. Maybe you need a fresh start in this season of your life or business. Steve tells a wonderfully personal story of growth, humility, patience, and perseverance. Do yourself a favor, listen and learn from this generous man who lives daily in the favor of God."

Dr. Gary Hewins, senior pastor of Community
Bible Church, Highlands, North Carolina

"If you are intent on creating a harmonious, profitable, and life-producing culture within your business, your organization, or your family, Steve's in-depth look at this modern-day anomaly called Chick-fil-A is a must-read."

Jeffrey Cranford, president of Links Players
International and senior pastor of Church at
the Red Door, Palm Desert, California

"This is a wonderfully engaging and compelling book. I couldn't put it down. Steve lets us see through his eyes the heart and soul of Chick-fil-A. This book is a tribute to enduring values and living and working for what matters most."

Dr. Crawford W. Loritts, Jr., author, speaker, and radio host; senior pastor of Fellowship Bible Church, Roswell, Georgia

COVERT COWS

and

Chick-fil-A®

Steve Robinson

Former Chief Marketing Officer for Chick-fil-A

NELSON
BOOKS

An Imprint of Thomas Nelson

Published in Nashville, Tennessee, by Nelson Books, an imprint of Thomas Nelson. Nelson Books and Thomas Nelson are registered trademarks of HarperCollins Christian Publishing, Inc.

Thomas Nelson titles may be purchased in bulk for educational, business, fund-raising, or sales promotional use. For information, please e-mail SpecialMarkets@ThomasNelson.com.

Library of Congress Cataloging-in-Publication Data

Names: Robinson, Steve, 1950- author.
Title: Covert cows and chick-fil-A : how faith, cows, and chicken built an iconic brand / Steve Robinson.
Description: Nashville : Thomas Nelson, 2019. |
Identifiers: LCCN 2018050292 (print) | LCCN 2019005426 (ebook) | ISBN 9781400213191 (e-book) | ISBN 9781400213160 (hardback)
Subjects: LCSH: Chick-Fil-A Corporation--History. | Branding (Marketing)--United States--History. | Fast food restaurants--United States--History. | Advertising--United States--History. | Businesspeople--United States.
Classification: LCC TX945.5.C4 (ebook) | LCC TX945.5.C4 R63 2019 (print) | DDC 647.9573--dc23
LC record available at https://lccn.loc.gov/2018050292

Printed in the United States of America

19 20 21 22 23 LSC 10 9 8 7 6 5 4 3 2 1

Contents

Forewords

If you asked me whether the Cows would have scribbled one misspelled phrase on a billboard had Chick-fil-A been a conventionally structured company at the mercy of shareholders or mega-franchisees, I'd say *slim chance*. The Cow campaign became an endearing part of American pop culture largely because of an independent, family-owned business armed with conviction.

While the creative team who conceived the idea gets much of the credit, the successful launch of the "Eat Mor Chikin" movement required great courage from a CMO who saw an original idea and approved it based on his instincts, without the benefit of focus groups or any kind of testing. Drawing on a reservoir of experience, Steve Robinson immediately recognized the power and scope of the idea and gave the Cows wings to fly (or, at least, shimmy up some billboards).

Few clients are willing to stick with one campaign for more than twenty years, even after it has proved successful. We were blessed to have a partner who listened to his gut (and a highly educated one, at that) time and time again. Steve and his team always showed up at meetings looking to be entertained, the fate of the ad often determined by the volume of Steve's infectious laugh. Every work session with Chick-fil-A was a joyous occasion, and all of us worked as a team in selecting the work that would keep the Cows fearlessly marching down the path of self-preservation and making advertising history.

As a leader, Steve was as respectful and inclusive with his own staff as he was with us. In our creative reviews, after we presented a dozen or so possible solutions, Steve would give each member of his team a chance to speak before he weighed in. He always listened intently and allowed open discussion, but we all knew it was his ultimate decision (fortunately for us, he made really good ones). Steve's approach not only set a tone of collaboration but also inspired us to always bring the very best ideas we were capable of producing. With Steve, it never felt like you were selling the work, but rather sharing something you were genuinely excited about with a friend.

Our relationship with Chick-fil-A was a paragon of the client–agency partnership, where graciousness and trust were always present at the table. Because of this uniquely collaborative spirit, fresh ideas flourished, the Cows never tired, and the world ate a whole lot more chicken.

Stan Richards
The Richards Group

....

In my world of management consulting, once or twice a decade you get to have an experience and relationship that reminds, inspires, and takes you back to the reasons you chose the career you did. My experience with Chick-fil-A and relationship with one of its most inspiring, transformational, and truly exceptional marketers, leaders, and friends, Steve Robinson, is one of those reasons. Steve was one of the original leaders that helped to bring to life and realize the vision born out of legendary business pioneer Truett Cathy's belief that there did not have to be a separation of business and humanity, purpose and dollars, and spirituality and growth.

For more than three decades, Steve led the creation, management, and relentless curation of one of the most iconic and beloved brands on the planet, using equal parts head and heart, intuition and analytics, and leadership and inspiration. As a top Chick-fil-A executive, Steve worked as hard at building the business and brand as he did the culture and his team. As a brand builder, Steve was a teacher, innovator, risk-taker, and true marketing pioneer. As a client, I truly learned what informed intuition meant and how Steve saw the world through both a data and human lens, which always led our teams to get to a collective better answer, regardless of the problem we were trying to solve together. As a friend, Steve continues to teach me about the importance of balance in all aspects of life, for with balance comes wisdom and a sense of peace.

Steve never wavered from his strong belief that Chick-fil-A would one day become one of the world's most beloved and powerful brands, while always admitting he could never make this a reality on his own. Steve always made sure that he had his executive leadership team aligned, his marketing leadership team empowered, his organization equipped, and the millions of raving fans ready to embrace both Chick-fil-A's amazing food and its incredible brand.

Covert Cows and Chick-fil-A does an incredible job of paralleling Steve's growth as a world-class marketer with the growth of a world-class brand and the growth of one of the most successful businesses in the fast casual industry. This is a book for students, teachers, marketers, entrepreneurs, dreamers and, most importantly, leaders who are truly committed to building a transcendent brand and marketing organization.

Covert Cows and Chick-fil-A is one of the finest books I have read that captures the history and legacy of both a business and a brand, while pushing the reader to constantly think about higher order purposes and ideas—and showing that they don't have to be in conflict with one another. Steve's ability to tell a story so vividly allows the reader to step through his life, Truett Cathy's life, and the building of one of the greatest, most iconic brands in the world. This is a must-read for anyone who dares to dream big, is seeking purpose in their life, has ambition, or wants a formula for business and life success (purpose and culture are great places to start).

Scott Davis,
Chief Growth Officer, PROPHET,
marketing and brand consultants

Introduction

Truett Cathy stood beside me on the sideline of the Georgia Dome with seventy-two thousand cheering college football fans surrounding us. For sixteen straight years, Truett, founder of Chick-fil-A, had stood on that field just before kickoff while plush Cows parachuted from the rafters, an inflatable Cow guided a blimp with an *Eat Mor Chikin* sign inside the dome, and often, his son Dan played the national anthem on his trumpet. The Chick-fil-A Peach Bowl had become something of a family affair, with fans, Cows, players, and coaches all together in the dome for a few hours of fun and football.

This game, December 31, 2012, was different. Truett was ninety-one years old, and I didn't know how many more bowl or Chick-fil-A Kickoff Games he might participate in. Also, we were deeply engaged in negotiations for Atlanta to be chosen as one of the host cities for the College Football Playoff (CFP) beginning after the 2014 season.

If Atlanta were to be selected, then the Chick-fil-A Bowl would host a CFP semifinal game every three years and two top-twenty teams in the other years. The National Championship game would also be in the mix for Atlanta. Chick-fil-A, including the Cows and our food, would become part of the experience for fans attending all seven of the CFP games, and our ads would be in heavy rotation on all seven of the national telecasts, introducing those renegade Cows to legions of new fans. Truett and I stood on the sideline and on the cusp of something altogether different and new for the Chick-fil-A brand.

I spoke loudly so he could hear me over the noise of the crowd. "Truett, your decision sixteen years ago made this possible," I said. He looked up, and I reminded him of the day when the Chick-fil-A executive committee was deadlocked on whether the company should become the first title sponsor of the Peach Bowl. Truett cast the deciding vote in favor and opened the door to marketing opportunities and partnerships with college football that catapulted Chick-fil-A to national brand status. In the intervening years, the number of stores had almost tripled to 1,683 (in 2012), and system-wide annual sales had grown eightfold to more than $4.6 billion.

We got a signal from the officials, and Truett walked out to the fifty-yard line for the coin toss with the captains from Clemson and LSU. He and I loved that moment, especially the energy of the cheering crowd while he stood among those huge college football players. Looking up at the tens of thousands in the stands, we both appreciated the impact and scale of the chain he had started forty-five years earlier. The customers visiting Chick-fil-A restaurants on a single day across the country could fill more than *thirty* Georgia Domes. But Truett didn't spend his time thinking about sales volume and customers in the aggregate. Big numbers didn't impress him. They were nothing but a scorecard, never his "why." He was more interested in the individual encounter—one customer face-to-face with one restaurant Operator or team member. For thirty-one years I watched Truett make thousands of those one-to-one connections. And believe me, I was one of them.

My role, as chief marketing officer and executive vice president at Chick-fil-A, was to provide the tools and the strategic architecture to build the Chick-fil-A brand. Truett provided the heart. I saw from my first day on the job that Truett had instincts, wisdom, and the grace for branding beyond anything I had seen or could imagine. Especially grace.

Nobody knew better than Truett that *grace* is the Chick-fil-A brand. We might attract new customers every day through marketing and advertising, but he insisted we maintain those relationships through grace that can take many forms in a fast-food restaurant: a friendly smile, eye contact, a personal connection, genuine interest in every person. He not only insisted on it, but he modeled and created a culture of grace.

If his business demonstrated grace and graciousness, then maybe in the process, people would discover the truth of what he believed. But he was not going to lead with his faith. He reminded us, Chick-fil-A is not a church or a ministry: "I'm not going to put scripture on packaging or on the bottom of cups. We're not going to put evangelical material in our restaurants. I want people to discover what we believe because of how we treat them. Jesus didn't say, 'I expect you to be a bullhorn.' He said, 'I expect you to be salt. I expect you to be light.'"

Being closed on Sundays was the most overt "pronouncement" Truett would make. When he stood in front of audiences and said, "I have never seen a conflict between biblical principles and good business practice," he was attempting to live out grace and truth—and grace came before truth. Through his business and his life, he wanted healthy relationships where he could influence a few hundred teenagers, eventually a few thousand campers every year, and then tens of thousands of young team members in restaurants. Those were opportunities he probably never dreamed would happen.

I saw alignment in his commitment and my desire for my spiritual walk. I saw hope for me to have a career where I would not be in conflict, theologically or in principle, with the man I was working for. Hope, in an environment where I could live out my biblical values. Where my career was not just a job but a platform to serve others and to serve Christ, not as an evangelist or a preacher or a teacher, but as a businessman attempting to live out the gospel of grace and truth.

Chick-fil-A is built on biblical values and principles that were fundamentally rooted in its founder and that play out through a business that serves and values people and tries to honor all. In 1946, Truett created this environment at his Dwarf Grill, and he carried it into Chick-fil-A restaurants and even to Chick-fil-A events.

Culture is the fertile ground that helps to grow a brand. A strong, clear, and understood culture sets up the growth of a great brand. A weak, unclear culture will always lead to a weak brand. Stated another way, a culture that is endearing to associates and customers results in an endearing and enduring brand. Conversely, a culture that is unsure of its emotional vision and values will never yield an endearing and enduring brand.

Early in my career, working with Texas Instruments, Six Flags Over Georgia, and Chick-fil-A, I operated in the paradigm that the most important things affecting my success in serving my employer were smart and innovative marketing, brand strategies, and programs. I was consumed by this dominant and hard-driving premise. And sure enough, those things *were* important and played major roles in the success I enjoyed. With time, however, I discovered something that could complement or even *trump* ideas and execution: *the culture of the business.*

The dominant strategies and initiatives that have helped to make Chick-fil-A what and who it is today grew out of the culture established by Truett Cathy and are described by its brand essence: "Where good meets gracious."

With this book I hope to honor God's favor not only on my life and my career but on Chick-fil-A as well. This is a story that none of us could have dreamed or orchestrated in our own strength or wisdom. At times, it was like an out-of-body experience, watching the events unfold.

I am so grateful for the privilege to have served Chick-fil-A, its Operators (restaurant franchisees), and Truett in a culture that proved to be fertile soil for growing a great brand. Along that journey, I discovered it was fertile soil not only for my professional growth but also my personal and spiritual growth.

This book is my story of that discovery and journey.

ONE

The Formation of a Brand

Great brands grow from great cultures, and as chief marketing officer at Chick-fil-A for almost thirty-five years, I was indeed operating in great cultural soil.

Truett Cathy had a sincere desire to honor God and have a positive influence on every person he came in contact with. Before the product and profits came relationships with people and with God. When Truett felt he had a biblical insight on an issue, whether it related to people or money or leadership, he tried to humbly and quietly apply that insight. Prudence. Patience. Hard work. Love. Forgiveness. Generosity. These values served Chick-fil-A well.

The year he passed away, 2014, the chain had grown to 1,887 restaurants with $5.7 billion in sales. In the subsequent two years, sales grew by another billion dollars per year, and the culture he created allowed people to continue to thrive. Today, nearly one hundred thousand people work throughout the Chick-fil-A chain, serving more than

3 million customers every day, or 1.1 billion per year. Its tremendous popularity is evident when a new store opens: people camp outside the night before to be among the first one hundred customers of a new restaurant because those customers receive free Chick-fil-A for a year.

Through the years, the leadership team established guiding principles that shaped how they made decisions—principles that were the ingredients of the culture. These provide the framework for the brand itself and for this book, and that framework begins with the Chick-fil-A Corporate Purpose:

> *To glorify God by being a faithful steward of all that is entrusted to us and to have a positive influence on all who come into contact with Chick-fil-A.*

This is our "why." And it's carried out even in the most iconic visual connected with Chick-fil-A: the beloved Cows. One of our former marketing consultants, Alf Nucifora, noted, "The [Cow] campaign offers an interesting insight into Chick-fil-A's corporate style." After noting that one of Chick-fil-A's strengths lies in their commitment to a decision or direction once it is created, "like their Corporate Purpose or Operator concept," he continued, "they don't waver. They don't shift. That is refreshing, and from a marketing standpoint, it can be very valuable, as you can see with the Cow campaign. They have resisted the urge to gussie it up, to change it, to get rid of it, or to do the wrong things to it."

The Corporate Purpose statement, created in 1982, grew out of a time of financial crisis when the national economy was in the midst of a serious recession and same-store sales fell for the first time ever. Capturing it in writing and disseminating it around the company kept our focus on why we were in business and on the deeply held beliefs that fed our culture.

Truett often talked about stewardship of talent, money, and influence, which belong to God who entrusts them to us. Serving as a steward rather than an owner of the assets gave Truett a freedom to express his generosity by sharing God's gifts with his associates and neighbors. He impacted many lives, and his model deeply affected me.

As Chick-fil-A grew, with the Corporate Purpose as our cultural foundation, we didn't think in terms of revolutionary initiatives for building the brand. Others might look at the Cow campaign, or college football, or the introduction of the grilled sandwich as strategic milestones, but we saw them as more than that. The real journey was moving from a sandwich-focused operational restaurant chain to an experiential brand, as we came to understand how Cathy family-style hospitality and relational marketing could be executed in a fast-food restaurant. Out of that understanding came our mission: "Be REMARKable." We wanted every customer's brand encounter to be remarkable, to leave an above-average, positive impression. To that end, we attempted to create experiences that people would want to talk about.

To achieve this mission, we created the Raving Fan Strategy,[1] which executed Operational Excellence, delivered Second-Mile Service, and activated Emotional Connections Marketing. These three major strategic pillars represent the operating strategy, and they are all designed to undergird restaurant Operators as they express and build the brand. And that last phrase is key—singular, in fact, in the fast-food industry. Chick-fil-A restaurant Operators serve as the primary expression of the brand as they meet customers at the front line. Only they can deliver the total Raving Fan experience.

Other brands rely on marketing and advertising to drive customers to restaurants. Chick-fil-A relies on the restaurant Operators and the teams they build to attract customers into their restaurants. Others drive; we attract. To make such a system succeed, Truett created a store-level financial model that generously favors the Chick-fil-A

Operator rather than the home office or the owners (which was Truett and is now the Cathy family, though they will tell you that God owns Chick-fil-A). This financial model attracts leaders who build a culture of true hospitality.

As I tell the story of the brand, almost every aspect of it begins with Truett's heart. He may have been the most humble man I ever knew, as well as the most generous and wise.

That's the basis of the culture, the soil that Chick-fil-A thrives in.

Truett instinctively knew what many professionals spend years learning: a successful brand builds a foundation on *relationships, relevance*, and *reputation*.

Relationships

Long before he created the Chick-fil-A Sandwich and decades before he opened the first Chick-fil-A restaurant, Truett Cathy was making friends and serving customers at his Dwarf Grill restaurant in Hapeville, Georgia. His genuine love created a space where people enjoyed good food together and employees truly felt like family. Truett and his brother Ben alternated working twelve-hour shifts six days a week. Truett, who was single when they opened, rented a room in a house next door and slept lightly. If he heard car tires crunching on the parking lot gravel, he got up and walked over to help his brother or the grill man. He developed *relationships*.

Relevance

Truett had selected the location deliberately. He didn't want to be lost in the crowd of small diners in Atlanta, which in 1946 included

Toddle Houses, Dutch Kitchens, and dozens of independents. The site he chose in downtown Hapeville was on US Highway 41, which connected Miami, Florida, to the Upper Peninsula of Michigan. In those pre-interstate highway days, thousands of travelers would pass his location every day. Also, Ford Motor Company was in the process of building its new Atlanta assembly plant across the road. Beginning in 1947, the plant would employ more than two thousand hourly workers. Every shift change would be an opportunity to serve workers coming and going. And the Atlanta Municipal Airport and thousands of airline employees were just around the corner. He focused on *relevance.*

Reputation

Truett and Ben borrowed as little money as possible, $6,600, to build their Dwarf Grill restaurant in 1946. They did much of the construction work themselves and bought used kitchen equipment to keep expenses down. Their total investment on opening day was $10,600.

"I can handle any problem but a financial problem," I heard Truett say many times. He avoided overextending, and he paid invoices quickly, patterning his life and his business after Proverbs 22:1: "A good name is to be chosen rather than great riches, loving favor rather than silver and gold" (NKJV). He understood *reputation.*

Truett Cathy didn't open the first Chick-fil-A restaurant until 1967, when he was forty-six years old. For the first two decades of his career he ran a mom-and-pop diner. That fact alone explains the difference between Chick-fil-A and so many other American brands. He was a restaurateur.

Truett also never got ahead of himself. He never let financial goals get in the way of personal relationships. In fact, Truett had an aversion to financial goals. To him, that would have been letting the tail wag the dog. When it came to business, his philosophy was to "climb with care and confidence," adding new restaurants slowly. He could have borrowed more money and grown the chain much faster. Money was never the limiting factor; banks were eager to lend money to Chick-fil-A. Rather, he would never grow faster than the chain could attract talent and build management systems. Disciplined growth allowed him to select Operators who shared his business philosophy and love for customers.

He kept borrowing to a minimum, and he never offered stock for sale. He never wanted the financial demands of bankers or shareholders to compromise decisions for his customers and employees. In essence, he didn't want to feel obligated to shareholders or lose control.

Most predominant American brands chase transactions, often through rapid growth. They borrow heavily to expand quickly. Businesses often focus on short-term results because of marketplace pressures. This is particularly true of publicly traded companies, which must report quarterly results to shareholders. Private companies sometimes fall into the same trap, foregoing the long-term opportunity to build a brand that people identify with and feel an emotional relationship with—a brand they cannot see themselves living without.

Roots of My Brand Experience

My first exposure to brand building came from my father, John B. Robinson, who, like Truett, started his business shortly after the end of World War II. Dad had grown up on his family's farm in Radnor, Ohio, northwest of Columbus, where his father raised Robinson Hybrid seed corn, a variety developed by my grandfather in consultation with Ohio State University. He could have stayed in the family business, but he was tired of Ohio winters and knew the growing season was longer in the South. So in 1948, soon after he married my mother, Martha Haynes, they moved to Foley, Alabama, in Baldwin County, where he and his brother Dale started their own hybrid seed corn business. Rather than attempting to build the Robinson Hybrid corn brand from scratch in the South, they chose to plant Funk hybrid seed corn because it had a marketing arm and a network of salesmen calling on seed corn wholesalers, farm supply distributors, and even foreign market distributors. It also led to higher yields for farmers. With more feed corn per acre than regular corn, it was a less expensive option for livestock.

Raising crops just ten miles north of the Gulf of Mexico, Dad envisioned getting a jump on the Midwest market by putting seed corn on barges headed north on the Mississippi River weeks before corn was ready for harvest in the Midwest. He succeeded, but Dad wasn't the only farmer who had seen the opportunity to get a head start. Over time the proliferation of hybrid corn in the South impacted the price of seed corn in the Midwest. In response (Dad thought, but we never really knew for sure), Congress passed the Farm Subsidy Bill. It propped up corn prices and paid property owners in parts of the Southeast to take acreage out of corn cultivation. In fact, it paid farmers more to plant trees or soybeans than Dad could pay to lease their land for his corn. Whatever Congress's intentions, the effect of the farm subsidy program was that seed corn producers across the South went out of business.

My dad was left with three options: find some other form of farming, declare bankruptcy, or sell his assets and find another line of work. He chose the third, selling his equipment for about ten cents on the dollar to his older brother, Cecil, who was still in the seed corn business in Ohio. Then he took the money and created a small manufacturing company. One semester short of a mechanical engineering degree from Ohio State University, he had always been drawn toward figuring out how to make equipment work better or more efficiently. He saw opportunities to design solutions to everyday problems and patented a hand nut-gathering tool and a burger press. He also designed (in partnership with an uncle) and manufactured an on-demand livestock watering fountain, and he even created all the machines and implements needed to produce his products.

Watching him, I grew up thinking I would become a mechanical engineer too. He had taught me well, working on machines and rebuilding cars. I enjoyed it. But my father's inventions didn't make much money. There were several years when he barely made ends meet. He drove thousands of miles, tracing and retracing the highways of Alabama and the Southeast, calling on his contacts and building relationships with wholesalers and store owners who liked him and his products. I sometimes traveled with him and saw firsthand how he struggled to sell little-known, niche-market products. He was in no position to build awareness and demand with potential customers, so his products didn't sell as well as others'. He never gave up, though. He was always ready to make the next call. Dad, like most entrepreneurs, was a perpetual optimist. And he had two of the three critical ingredients for brand success: *relationships* and *reputation*. What he didn't have was *relevance*—his potential users were just not aware of his quality products.

As I thought about how I could help, I realized that retail products with a recognizable brand sold better because of their perceived value. My thoughts at that time might not have been this strategic, but I soon learned the importance of a "brand promise," or a perception that one brand is better than another or better than a generic option: customers were willing to pay a premium for its higher perceived value.

If my dad had turned sour like Willy Loman in *Death of a*

Salesman, any good thoughts I had about selling might have withered. Instead, Dad's everlasting optimism allowed my curiosity around sales, marketing, and brands to bloom in a safe space. Even as a teenager in the 1960s, I began to connect the dots. I was growing up in the fifties and sixties, when Proctor & Gamble, Kraft, General Foods, Unilever, and others were creating identities for multiple products led by brand managers. It was the era of brand development. During my junior year in high school, I decided not to study engineering in college but to pursue a degree in marketing. I had come to a simple conclusion: nothing happens until someone sells something. I wanted a career being that "someone."

Two Men of the Greatest Generation

My father and Truett Cathy were part of the Greatest Generation, men who were hardworking, persevering, and incredibly loyal. My father treated all his employees with respect and would give you the shirt off his back. If he had any failing, it was that he did that too often. Like lost puppies, people who needed a break were attracted to him.

Truett, too, was incredibly respectful of everyone, no matter their station in life or ethnicity. The first time I walked into his Dwarf House restaurant in 1980, I noticed the diversity of his team: women, men, black, white. And I learned that most of them had been working with Truett for many years, some of them for decades.

To Truett, every customer, every Operator, every staff member, and every team member was important, and the loss of a single one bothered him. He was constantly seeking opportunities for new relationships, often with food and hospitality. He would meet someone and invite them to a meal in his home, calling his wife, Jeannette, at the last minute to say he had a guest, or guests, coming with him. The restaurant business Truett built became an extension of the genuine hospitality that he and Jeannette offered at home. When my wife, Dianne, and I visited Truett and Jeannette just months before he passed away, Truett was in a weakened state—yet he asked us to stay for dinner.

Truett truly had a desire to honor God and be a positive influence on every person he came in contact with. He did not think, *How can I create a great brand culture?* He simply did what came naturally to him. He made promises that his customers came to trust, and those promises continue to form the foundation of the Chick-fil-A brand.

More than sixty years after Truett started out in the restaurant business, his pastor asked him what advice he would leave for those who manage Chick-fil-A. Truett responded, "Keep on doing business the right way, and always take care of your customers."

No complex architecture. No lists or graphics. The advice came from the Bible. It was essentially, love God and love your neighbor. Do these, and everything else falls into place. By living those words himself, Truett created a culture of love, respect, trust, and grace that has allowed Chick-fil-A to thrive.

Like my father, though, long before Chick-fil-A became the beloved brand it is today, Truett faced a point when he had to reconsider the direction of his business career. For my father, Washington politics killed the hybrid seed corn business in the South with the activation of the Farm Subsidy Bill. For Truett, the death of his brother Ben, a restaurant fire, and colon surgery led him to reconsider his life's purpose.

He had opened his Dwarf Grill in 1946 with his brother Ben. Then in 1948, he married his childhood sweetheart, Jeanette McNeil. The three of them ran the restaurant together until Ben died in an airplane crash in 1949. Though Truett had lost his brother and his business partner, he and Jeanette persevered with a vision of owning a chain of diners. In 1951, he opened his second restaurant but almost immediately regretted the decision. With two restaurants, he couldn't be with his customers all the time. The idea of relationships with customers was real to him, not an abstract notion. He had capable managers at both restaurants, but when managers had problems they couldn't solve, they called Truett, whose time was then split between the two restaurants.

Fire destroyed the second restaurant in February 1960, and Truett was not carrying enough insurance to rebuild it without borrowing money. He took out a loan, but before construction began, his doctor found polyps in his colon and scheduled surgery. Though there was no cancer, Truett had a terrible allergic reaction to the anesthesia and stayed in the hospital for two weeks. Six months later his doctor found more polyps and told Truett that he required a second surgery. This was a pivotal moment for Truett.

"I was thirty-eight years old, and I did not expect to come home alive," he wrote in his book *Eat Mor Chikin: Inspire More People*. Though his wife reassured him, "God isn't finished with your life yet. I don't think He's going to take you," the experience changed him. He said,

> In those moments I came to realize that the material things I had acquired, the success I had enjoyed with the Dwarf House, meant nothing. What mattered was my relationships with Jeannette, [our children] Dan, Bubba, Trudy, my friends, and most of all, my relationship with God. I experienced a new peace in the car that morning [going to the hospital], knowing that whether I lived or died I would be with God. . . .
>
> I learned the true value of life and was changed by that understanding. Certain things happen in life that strengthen our faith

> and remind us of our need to put our lives in the hands of the Lord. I came out of the hospital a new creation, prepared to take on whatever life dealt, for I knew God would be with me.[2]

After he recovered, Truett forged ahead and designed the new Forest Park Dwarf House as a self-serve fast-food restaurant, a new concept in 1961. When it opened, his customers disliked the reduced personal contact so much that he chose to close the restaurant in a matter of months. He leased the building to Ted Davis, who ironically used it to open Atlanta's first Kentucky Fried Chicken franchise. (God does have a sense of humor!)

Truett then poured all his energy into the single operation, the original Dwarf House. One restaurant and one owner on-site, working alongside employees to serve customers, was an experience that would strongly influence the Chick-fil-A franchise model later. It was there he also established the foundations of the Chick-fil-A sandwich:

- He created and perfected the recipe for the original boneless breast of chicken sandwich over a period of five years.
- He realized the sandwich was good enough to build a restaurant menu around.
- He created a unique, memorable name for the sandwich that clearly identified the product and communicated its quality.

During the next few years, he experimented with the recipe. He initially called it a "chicken steak sandwich," and his Dwarf House customers were his focus group. As the recipe neared perfection, he added those two crucial pickles whose sour tartness complemented the slight sweetness of his breading, and he continued to work on the name. Since he was using the best part of the chicken, a boneless breast—the filet—he changed the name to Chick Filet. Then he added the capital A, which to him implied the highest quality, and Chick-fil-A was born.

Truett planned to license the sandwich to other restaurant owners, so he purposely designed simple preparation procedures that could be repeated in various locations. Then he introduced the sandwich at the 1964 Southeastern Restaurant Trade Association convention, walking away with licensing agreements for fifty restaurants.

But Truett didn't leave the marketing of his new sandwich to chance. He and Jeanette traveled to towns around the South, talking up the Chick-fil-A sandwich and giving away his now-famous creation, the "Be Our Guest" card, that could be redeemed for a free sandwich at the Dwarf House. They were successful in their endeavors. Even Waffle House, the iconic Atlanta-based restaurant chain, became a licensee. Then, when the Houston Astrodome was completed the following spring, the Chick-fil-A sandwich was sold on opening day, making it an instant hit.

Demand for Consistent Quality: Opening Chick-fil-A

Great brands become great when they are consistent on every key level of execution. A bottle of Coca-Cola tastes the same in New York or in Shanghai. The bottle itself was designed to be distinctive enough to identify in the dark or at the bottom of an ice-filled cooler. Harley-Davidson determined that its sound was important, so it protected that sound, even in the law. You don't have to see a Harley to know one is coming.

I am convinced that Truett, too, had a sense of this need for consistency. In time, however, he began to notice that as simple as the Chick-fil-A sandwich recipe was, preparing it consistently in every location was not easy. Instead of cooking the chicken immediately before serving, some restaurants were cooking a day's worth of chicken in the morning and keeping it warm until it was sold. Or worse, on game day at the Astrodome they were cooking all the chicken early, then refrigerating it and later rewarming it during the game.

When the sandwich began to receive negative reviews, Truett knew he had lost control of his creation. He decided he had to be able to control the quality of his sandwich, so he began to undo the licensing deals.

At about the same time, his sister Gladys, who had a card shop in Greenbriar Center, Atlanta's first indoor shopping mall, suggested that Truett open a restaurant in the mall and feature his Chick-fil-A sandwich. The mall only offered table-service restaurants, but she thought people might prefer another option, one that wouldn't require taking a long break from shopping or work . . . something they might even want to eat as they walked the mall.

Always the entrepreneur, Truett approached mall management with the idea. They initially didn't like the idea of selling sandwiches from a counter inside the mall because of potential odors and accumulating waste. He politely persisted, though, and soon signed a lease for a thirteen-foot-wide space. His next step led to a serendipitous relationship with Jimmy Collins, an independent restaurant and kitchen designer, who later would play a vital role in the growth of Chick-fil-A as he ran the operations of the chain. Jimmy helped Truett design this first restaurant, which opened in 1967. It covered less than four hundred square feet of space yet generated more than $180,000 in sales during Truett's first year. In 1967 dollars, that was not too shabby.

Leasing and building out mall space required much less up-front capital than building on the street, and the mall-only strategy connected Chick-fil-A with a pleasant experience—a visit to the mall. Enclosed shopping malls were new to the suburban scene, and Chick-fil-A Operators enjoyed a significant "image rub" from being in an upscale retail environment. Customers who did not know the brand or the product assumed Chick-fil-A offered high quality because the restaurants were surrounded by other high-quality tenants that had been vetted by the mall developer. As part of the experience, Chick-fil-A became a shopping treat.

Chick-fil-A Operators delivered on that promise. Truett expected operational excellence from day 1, and Operators responded with great food in a clean, wholesome environment.

Truett's first marketing outreach from the earliest Chick-fil-A restaurant continues to be one of the most effective: giving away the food. In the beginning, he offered bite-sized samples at the lease line, then he added his tried and tested Be Our Guest cards to the mix. The act of giving and receiving, be it a sample bite or a Be Our Guest Chick-fil-A sandwich card, created an emotional connection. The recipient received something free—a gift with no strings attached—and experienced a delicious product. Truett knew if people sampled his product, they would buy it, and he was right. This idea became the inspiration for the early mall-focused advertising line, "Taste it. You'll love it for good!"

Truett encouraged Operators to give away forty BOGs every day. "Don't do it hit or miss," he said. "Invest a little all the time, sample all the time, distribute BOGs all the time." He instinctively understood the value of consistent, habitual marketing investment.

Smile!

As more Chick-fil-A restaurants opened, Truett enjoyed engaging with guests, and he encouraged Operators and team members to do the same. Jimmy Collins, Chick-fil-A's first chief operating officer, told this story to illustrate that point. He later wrote it down for me. It is a classic.

> On Grand Opening day of Paramus Mall, as usual Truett was at the lease line offering samples of Chick-fil-A to shoppers.
>
> As he returned to the kitchen to get a fresh plate of samples, he said to me, "That girl is not smiling." He pointed to Martha. She seemed to be having a bad day and certainly was not smiling.
>
> I went to Martha and told her she was to smile at the customers and walked away.
>
> When Truett returned for another plate of samples, he said, "She is still not smiling."
>
> I said, "I will see that she does it this time."
>
> But instead, Truett stopped me and said, "I'll take care of it."
>
> I was puzzled. What did he intend to do that he thought would be better than the instructions I was giving her? I watched.
>
> Truett walked up to Martha and said, "Why is it that every time I look at you, you are smiling?"
>
> She did give him a little smile, but it didn't last. I thought, That is not going to work, but kept my eye on her and Truett.
>
> The next time he passed her as he went into the kitchen, he said, "There you are smiling again." She gave him a bigger smile that lasted a little longer. By this time I was giving my full attention to watching the two of them.
>
> Truett would often turn from sampling to smile at Martha. Every time he did, she would smile!
>
> Soon Martha was wearing a big beautiful smile that lasted the rest of the day.
>
> That day I learned a great lesson of how the use of personal power is so much more effective than position power. I learned from a master, Truett Cathy. Truett never told her what to do,

> but he clearly and simply made it attractive for her to do what he expected. As I thought about it, I realized that was how Truett led all of us.[3]

Truett's approach to hospitality with customers and employees was always the same—personal and genuine. And it always started with a smile.

TWO

Learning and Implementing Brand Strategy

I was a senior at Foley High School in December 1967 and, of course, knew nothing of the opening of Chick-fil-A in Greenbriar Center. I had just returned from spending a year as an American Field Service exchange student in Christchurch, New Zealand, an amazing experience for a South Alabama teenager.

When I graduated from high school in the spring of 1968, my family couldn't do much to help financially with college costs. So I enrolled in Faulkner State Junior College (now part of Coastal Alabama Community College) that fall, where the work-study program allowed me to earn money working on a landscape crew. I also worked in general construction during the summers. But as a bonus, I was able to make the Faulkner State baseball team as a walk-on, my last fling participating in team sports.

One night my teammates invited me to join them at a youth rally in Mobile, where David Wilkerson was speaking. Wilkerson was a preacher who had gone to New York City in 1958 to minister to seven gang members on trial for murder. He stayed and ultimately helped thousands of kids on the New York City streets to change their lives, kids who were overcome by poverty, crime, and drugs. He later wrote *The Cross and the Switchblade* about his experience, and the book sold millions of copies, making a huge impact on teenagers across the country. As it turned out, I would be one of them.

I had grown up in a going-to-church environment that, to me, seemed to be mostly about rules. At least that's the way I felt as a teenager. Performance—rules for what you do and what you don't do, who you hang out with and who you don't hang out with, what you say and what you don't say, what you drink and what you don't drink. Don't get me wrong; this attitude probably served me well and kept me out of trouble. But by the time I was a sophomore in college, I found myself having no hunger or joy in my spiritual walk. I experienced seasons of guilt because I had bad thoughts, said bad things, or behaved poorly, and I couldn't erase those things from my life or my mind. It was all about my performance. And I was frustrated.

Wilkerson's way of working with young people in New York, I learned that night in Mobile's coliseum, was to first deal with their soul, their spirit, and help them understand how to build a life—from the inside out—around the reality of living as a Christian. I listened to his story and the power of the resurrection—not just Christ's resurrection, but resurrection in the lives of those kids in New York City who were turning their lives over to Christ. He explained that the gospel is about grace, not rules. We don't earn our salvation; it's a gift because of the finished work of Christ's death and resurrection.

What?!

Although I had heard that message of grace before, I'd never fully understood it was for me. And I thought, *This is what's missing from my life. I can't operate in this constant struggle of trying to deal with my shortcomings and sense of separation from God by myself. I have bad thoughts and behavior that create a relational chasm between me and God. I don't really KNOW Him. And nothing I seem to do can bridge this separation.* It was as if Christ called my name and, as a popular worship song says, "I walked out of the grave." *My* grave. I gave my life to Christ that night in Mobile, Alabama. I wanted to be part of His life and the reality of His redemption for me.

Reflecting on that time, I think of a statement by Dr. Charles Swindoll: "Conversion to Christ is the initial downbeat to an entire magnum opus, which God composes of our lives."[4] The reality of this only became clear years later, and quite frankly, my recognition of it became louder as I wrote this book.

That experience began my long journey to understand biblical grace. Years later, when Dianne and I were married, we became involved in churches with solid biblical teaching, and my understanding of the gospel of grace grew clearer. I studied the stories of Christ's interaction with people through the lens of the apostle John's statement that He came in grace and truth. He always led with grace. He didn't prejudge the people He interacted with. It didn't matter if it was the harlot, or the woman with an issue of blood, or Zacchaeus up in the tree, or a tax collector named Matthew. Story after story, He led with grace. He accepted people for who they were and willingly went to their dinner parties. He didn't want to leave anyone behind. More times than not, He shared truth only as they asked Him questions or after He had developed a relationship with them.

That night in Mobile changed my life, my purpose, and my worldview.

I finished junior college and transferred to Auburn University, where I majored in marketing and worked at a boarding house for my meals. I loved Auburn. Still do. I've been buying season football tickets since Bo Jackson was a freshman! My two years there flew by.

Early in my senior year, I stopped by unannounced to see the dean in the College of Business, Dr. George Horton, a transparent and engaging leader. I had started interviewing for jobs, and most of the opportunities were sales jobs. I mean road sales. Road warriors. Pharmaceuticals, power companies, supply companies, tech companies like Xerox. I had been there and done that with my dad, and it wasn't the career that excited me. I told Dean Horton that I was attracted to the communications and brand-building side of marketing and asked if he had any ideas.

"If I were to consider grad school," I said, "where should I go?"

Without hesitation, he said, "I can tell you three places you ought to consider. Given what you want to do, you don't need a traditional MBA. You ought to consider a master's with an advertising and communications focus."

"Okay," I said. "Where?"

"Either Columbia, Stanford, or Northwestern's Medill School of Journalism and Advertising. And I would probably recommend Medill, because virtually all their staff are former practitioners, and every quarter, you're going to have a practical project with an agency or client."

He volunteered to call Dean Vernon Fryberger at Medill and learned that the next year's class was already filled, but Dr. Horton persuaded him to grant me an interview.

The previous spring, a great friend and Auburn FarmHouse fraternity brother, Jerry Batts, had set up a blind date for me with Dianne Keen, whose brother, Bobby, was one of the chapter's founders. We hit it off, two kids from rural Alabama, me from Foley and her from Billingsley. When I decided to go to graduate school, I didn't want to go without her, so I proposed. She said yes, and her parents said yes, so Dianne and I drove up to Northwestern with my parents. I met with Dean Fryberger and members of his faculty.

"I can't make any promises," he told me as we left, "and the odds are against you, but I'll let you know."

A short while later I got a letter from him saying, "You're in." Amazing! But now I had another problem: I didn't have any money. This was before the day of cheap student loans, and I had to have ten thousand dollars for tuition within weeks. (Looking back, what a bargain!) Though my dad had not been able to help pay for most of my undergraduate education, he offered to cosign on a loan, pledging the assets of his business as collateral. And the local bank granted the loan.

Dianne and I graduated from Auburn on June 6, 1972, and were married four days later. Two weeks later we loaded up a U-Haul behind my '63 Ford Galaxie and headed to Northwestern. There were thirty-six members in my Medill class, and I was number thirty-six. I was the only one from south of the Mason-Dixon Line, and boy, did I hear about my accent. *What accent?* They were the ones with the accent.

Dianne got a job as a secretary in the behavioral science department of the MBA program, earning enough money to pay for our room and board. We were living in Evanston, north of Chicago, but we didn't have money to enjoy much of the city. Occasionally, though, we would pack hot dogs and go to a White Sox or Cubs game (we were only eight miles from Wrigley Field).

In class, my classmates and I were studying media strategy, creative strategy development, campaign development, and public relations. Simultaneously, we were working on a campaign project for either an agency or a client directly, immediately applying what we had learned in the classroom—writing campaign strategy, creative briefs, creative development, media strategy, and media plans for a client every quarter.

Because my professors had been practitioners, they brought a reality to the classroom that made the Northwestern experience special—very powerful and marketable. That's still their philosophy today.

The work was nonstop for four straight quarters. We spent long hours preparing our case studies beyond our normal classroom work, working in small teams with one person leading creative, another doing media, and another drafting strategy. Teams competed with each other in an effort to mimic the real world.

One quarter my team created a campaign for a protein-based shampoo product. Our strategy created a point of difference for the brand by communicating the virtues of milk in the shampoo.

Another project was for the kids' space in McDonald's, and that experience led to a job interview with their agency (how ironic).

After a year at Northwestern, I graduated with the tools I needed to think about and document a brand strategy, develop a marketing plan that flows out of that brand strategy—it's not the other way around—and plan all the communications that flow out of the marketing vision.

They taught me how to think strategically. Undergrad school at Auburn gave me the traditional academic experience of topical silos: studying consumer behavior and research, media, pricing, economics, finance, and accounting. Northwestern put it all together and showed how these silos fit into the broader construct of building a brand, a marketing plan to support the brand, and then the communication strategies within that. Dr. Horton had given me great counsel.

Creating a Wholesome Environment

While I was learning branding strategies from some of the finest marketing minds in the world, Truett was implementing his intuitive, personal vision for growing Chick-fil-A. Three business decisions were particularly instrumental to its success. They set the foundation for the workplace environment in Chick-fil-A stores.

One of those was the decision to close on Sundays: it set the tone for what was important. A day set aside for him and all who were part of Chick-fil-A to rest, be with family, and worship, if they so chose. Sales and profits were not everything.

Another crucial decision was the creation of a unique store-leadership financial model that is still used today and is not likely to be replicated by another fast-food brand despite the obvious positive impacts it brings to the business and the brand.

Truett wanted personally engaged leadership in every Chick-fil-A restaurant, and the only way to guarantee that was to create a financial model in which each franchisee would operate only one restaurant, which meant each restaurant had to generate healthy income through strong sales with long-term growth potential, allowing the Operator to sustain that business year after year. Unlike most other franchise chain leadership, Truett was not looking to create a portfolio of restaurants with great locations that supported lower-caliber sites. Each restaurant had to be a winner. Also, he was not looking for franchise investors; he sought talented restaurant leaders to own and operate restaurants, no matter their finances. Thus, he created the Chick-fil-A franchise agreement, which remains basically unchanged today, around these key components:

- No up-front franchise fee. Operators make a five thousand dollar refundable commitment (changed to ten thousand dollars in 2016).
- No up-front capital investment by the franchisee (this is all Chick-fil-A's responsibility)
- Only one restaurant per franchisee (exceptions came much later)

Other fast-food brands require their franchisees to invest more than a million dollars to open a restaurant, usually in the form of an up-front brand rights fee, plus capital dollars for site, facility, and equipment. Not Chick-fil-A, which selects the site, builds the restaurant, then purchases and places all the equipment. Once underway, the franchisee pays Chick-fil-A, Inc., 15 percent of its sales for the use of the brand and for all the brand's support systems. After the Operator pays all the expenses of running the restaurant, profits are split evenly with Chick-fil-A, Inc. Chick-fil-A's half is categorized as an "additional Operator charge." The other half is the Operator's income.

The deal Truett created in 1967 is incredibly generous, and it is a win-win. This ingenious model has never been changed, except to increase the guaranteed base draw. It builds trust with Operators. More than anything else, the franchise agreement motivates the Operator to take care of customers, take care of details, manage profits and losses, attract great people to work in the restaurant, and grow the business. It allowed Truett the opportunity to replicate himself so that every Chick-fil-A Operator has the spirit and drive of an entrepreneur, genuine love for customers and employees, a commitment to develop young people, and the gift of hospitality. Because the restaurant's employees work for the Operator, it also generates longer store-level employee retention, and thus, more opportunities for personal and professional development for their team members.

In 2018, there were approximately two thousand Chick-fil-A restaurant Operators. The continued success of the brand requires each of them to regularly assess whether their leadership is producing the customer, business, and brand performance specified in their agreement with Chick-fil-A. And for staff, particularly those focused on Operator selection, are they holding future Operator candidates up to the light of Truett's original intentions for a Chick-fil-A Operator? Because, ultimately, the Chick-fil-A brand rises and falls on the leadership style and values of the restaurant Operators. In the end, do they value what Truett valued? Quality attracts quality, so Operator selection is the most important decision made at Chick-fil-A.

In 2017, the average Chick-fil-A freestanding restaurant had sales 70 percent higher than the average McDonald's location and four times that of an average KFC location. Approximately 450,000 customers visit the average Chick-fil-A restaurant every year—some 1,700 each day. Operators develop effective leadership teams to manage volumes at that level, with the full intent of keeping those leaders for years. Some of their staff stay a long time because they aspire to be an Operator and they know one of the best ways to achieve that dream is to learn and be around a high-performing Operator.

To be effective, leadership teams must be diverse. Some team members are gifted in hospitality, others have a community outreach relationship or a marketing mind-set, and still others show their talent producing fresh food in the kitchen. Every restaurant needs leaders who are strong in operations and/or accounting to help run the restaurant, keep the books, and manage inventory. They also will have critical shift leaders for morning, midday, and evening. But the crucial, consistent "glue"? The Operator, who is the on-site leader and coach, engaged with the leaders, walking the floor and connecting with customers, and watching the performance of their team. They're focused on the same things Truett focused on when he walked around the dining room at the Dwarf House. Chick-fil-A is able to do all this because of its financial relationship with the Operator, which is profitable enough for the Operator to afford to invest in great leaders and high-caliber employees.

Customers have a better experience and a more consistent

experience at Chick-fil-A restaurants across the country because the company attracts high-caliber Operators who then attract high-caliber leaders and team members. And because their team-member turnover is less than one-third the industry average, Operators can afford to invest in their employees' training and development. When people learn that I worked at Chick-fil-A, the question they ask most often is, "How do you get such great people to work in the restaurants? The level of attention, caring, and service is amazingly consistent." The answer goes back to the store leadership model that Truett created with the Operator deal. It worked with the first restaurants he opened, and it has only improved over the decades.

Another key characteristic Truett sought in Operators was a strong drive to always improve. He was never satisfied unless he could say, "I got a sales increase in the Dwarf House this year." Though money wasn't his prime motivator, it was a scorecard showing that he and his team were doing the right things to earn support from current and new customers.

Chick-fil-A strives to select Operators with that same drive, utilizing the healthy tension of the motivated, independent businessperson who wants to grow sales and profits every year in partnership with the parent brand, which owns all the assets. The company can set a high bar on performance expectations and quality standards, and if there's an elongated track record of underperformance, they can make a change; people are standing in line to become an Operator.

The business model of highly compensated, highly motivated Operators who are in business for themselves but not by themselves became a foundation of the chain's success. Chick-fil-A could not do the things it has done in the restaurants and with the brand if not for the leadership talent in every restaurant. That, quite frankly, is the biggest point that competing chains cannot recreate.

Truett's motivation was clear: "I'm not interested in your money. I'm interested in your ability." After decades of observing great Operators, I believe Truett looked for two key traits:

- Their ability to attract, develop, and keep great people
- Their passion, or their "fire in the belly," as I like to label it. He looked for Operators who were never content with the status quo, who were always looking to improve food consistency, service, and sales.

Truett's experience owning the Dwarf House continues as the model for the Chick-fil-A chain. Unlike other franchise operations, Truett limited ownership to a single restaurant per franchisee, except in unusual circumstances. Franchisees would not be overseeing multiple managers at multiple locations. They would be in their own stores—in the dining room, the kitchen, or behind the counter—or out in their community, just as Truett had been for twenty-one years before starting Chick-fil-A.

The third significant decision Truett made (to affect the workplace environment) was to create and implement the Chick-fil-A Team Member Scholarship program in 1973, the same year I was graduating from Northwestern. Truett was drawn to the vigor of young minds and wanted to attract college students to his company, and the scholarship program gave restaurant employees who met certain benchmarks a one thousand dollar scholarship to pay for college expenses. The goal, like the Operator agreement, was to encourage team members to make a longer-term commitment to Chick-fil-A. The program, the first of its kind in the fast-food industry, became a powerful recruiting "extra" to help Operators attract and keep high-achieving teenagers.

Marketing Calculators and Dolphin Shows

With my hard-earned master's degree in hand, I directed my energies to finding employment back in the South. I pressed hard for opportunities with companies like Coca-Cola, Delta, Six Flags, Texas Instruments, and Frito-Lay. Though I received many rejection letters, some of which Dianne still has, Texas Instruments showed interest because they were gearing up a consumer marketing division to support a new line of handheld calculators. In fact, they were leaders in the space. But they were engineers, not experts in marketing, so they were hiring brand managers and communications people to build a consumer marketing department. They needed some young guns, and I fit the bill.

Texas Instruments (TI) was marketing directly to engineers and architects, mathematicians, students, chemists, and other technical professionals, and they offered me my first job—to help them market their scientific calculators to those targeted audiences. We relied on direct mail and trade journals, a skill set I had not acquired at Northwestern, where we dealt with building and marketing consumer brands with more traditional platforms and channels of distribution. So this continued my education.

I quickly learned how to use segmented media and direct mail, how to build direct mail lists, and how to calculate returns on investment per thousand reached through circulation or delivery. I was tutored on how to develop creative content that would solicit an immediate response. The experience was like another year in graduate school, in a one-to-one platform talking directly to the engineer, the math student, the architect, and others with similar interests.

At the same time, TI was responding to new entries to the market by driving down the cost and prices of their calculators, even though we were selling more product than they could manufacture. As the young brand guy, I thought we should be adding value to the technology and positioning ourselves as the premium-priced brand. After all, we were the early-entry brand, the preemptive technology leader, and we were learning how to crack the niche, high-end tech markets. Unfortunately, we often left bags of mail sitting on the mailroom floor because we had lowered prices despite the demand we were experiencing. It drove me nuts.

After a year of this, I was still an underling by a long shot, but I was engaged in a healthy debate with my supervisor and others over the company's vision for this segment of the business.

Then the telephone rang. Dan Howell, director of marketing for Six Flags Over Texas (SFOT), was on the line with an opportunity. Six Flags had entered into an agreement with the City of Arlington to manage the Seven Seas theme park next door to Six Flags. They needed a sales and promotions manager. Would I be interested?

Dan quickly explained that the relationship with Arlington and Seven Seas was only guaranteed for the 1974 season. The company did not own the park. They were on a management contract, so he could not promise a commitment beyond 1974. But if I was interested, I could come out on Saturday and spend the day exploring it.

I had high regard for Dan, a Medill grad with previous brand management experience. And his brother, Bob, was a close friend and Northwestern classmate. So, of course, I was interested.

In just a few hours, the Six Flags marketing team showed me a laboratory of marketing work and learning. Theirs was truly a marketing- and brand-driven business. The contrast to the engineering culture at TI could not have been more stark. I would be reporting to the director of marketing for Seven Seas with mentoring support from the Six Flags staff.

At the end of that Saturday visit, Dan offered me a job that would double my income and include a company car but, as he had said, offered no guarantees beyond the first season.

I couldn't pass up the potential for growth and new challenges. In addition to Dan, Six Flags, Inc., vice president of marketing George Delanoy and SFOT sales and promotions manager Jim Pemberton became friends and great mentors. I brought my TI experience, with its direct marketing to target audiences, and applied it to school, church, and tour groups. We developed a corporate benefits package that companies could offer as perks to their staff: the Six Flags Funseekers Club, which succeeded so well at Seven Seas and SFOT that it was replicated at all the Six Flags parks, as were other direct marketing programs. We filled the park with 375,000 visitors the summer of 1974, and at home, Dianne and I had a new visitor too: our beautiful daughter Jennifer Joy Robinson was born.

The morning of Joy's arrival, Dianne told me she thought it was time to go to the hospital. Hard-charging as I was, I dressed for work—coat, tie, the whole bit—in case it was a false alarm. When we arrived at Presbyterian Hospital, more than twenty women were in the maternity ward being prepped for deliveries—so many that Dianne had to be prepped in the hallway behind a screen! After the nurses had been watching her for two or three hours, the doctor examined her and said, "Get this woman a room! She's going to have a baby!" So finally I loosened my tie, and a few hours later, our first child, Joy, came into the world, along with the thrill, excitement, and responsibility of such an incredible gift from God. Of course, I had questions for myself: *How am I going to step up to this challenge? This responsibility?* You don't know how you'll answer those questions until you experience the reality of the birth of a child. God uses children to reveal and shape your character. Children are both a blessing and a test.

Most of the day-to-day responsibility for Joy fell to Dianne. She made the decision from the beginning that she would stay home with our children while I built my career. She allowed me to focus on my work because I knew she was with Joy and she was incredibly supportive of what I was doing.

Seven Seas, on the other hand, was a ninety-minute commute each way. On top of that, we had park hours on weekends, plus special events and concerts into the night. I wasn't home much, but Dianne never complained.

Then the City of Arlington chose not to make any additional investments in the Seven Seas guest experience, so the management contract began to look like a one-year transactional relationship after all. But the contract stipulated that if our work continued past year one, then the city would be obligated to invest capital to refresh the park and add more attractions. I hoped we might have a two- or three-year gig, and I could continue to learn from the Six Flags organization. I loved the Six Flags experience and the theme-park business—the adrenaline that came with the instant feedback of daily attendance, consumer marketing, and retail marketing, all rolled into one brand. Six Flags marketing and management leaders mentored me, investing time to guide me through strategic and tactical marketing issues as well as higher-level management of the business.

At the end of the season, the City of Arlington announced that it had made a new agreement with the founder of Sea World to manage Seven Seas, ending its relationship with Six Flags. Our general manager called me into his office, graciously laid out a severance package, and said at the end of the week my assignment was over. Just like that, I was out of a job.

I drove home playing out the whole thing in my mind—the decision to leave a stable job at Texas Instruments for a gamble. I knew that it might last for only a year. But now we had a child and a mortgage, and Dianne had paid such a price. We had saved some money, and the severance package would last a couple of months, but we were still sleeping on the pullout sofa.

I walked into the house with the news, and Dianne wasn't fazed. She hugged me and said, "God will provide." With her calm, stable influence at a time when we didn't know what would happen with my job and my career—she was a rock.

I still cried.

Learning to Trust God

Dianne was right. My unanticipated sabbatical did not last long: less than two weeks! Six Flags called with a new opportunity.

The company was opening smaller tourist attractions around the country, including the Movieland Wax Museum near Disneyland in California. More than a million patrons visited Movieland annually, and that success inspired the company to build a similar attraction, Stars Hall of Fame, near Disney World in Orlando. They hired me as sales and promotion manager, and for three years we enjoyed success. Stars Hall of Fame sat right next to Sea World, and with two hundred wax sculptures of stars placed in about a hundred built-out sets of classic movie scenes, we drew movie lovers of all ages.

At home, Dianne provided so much support with her encouragement, patience, and complete commitment to Joy and me, and I sought to support my family by seeking the counsel of other men. I'm a firm believer that iron sharpens iron (Proverbs 27:17). For me, that means engaging with other men who have demonstrated over a long period of time spiritual discernment, discipline, and submission to the Holy Spirit. They have proven their ability to lead, discipline, and develop people, even if it's not directly through a business. They speak truth, even when it's hard. Put another way, they are respectful truth-tellers.

Other than my dad, the first men who stepped into my life in this way were strong high school basketball and baseball coaches: Ivan Jones, Denzel Hollis, and Lester Smith. These coaches by their countenance, discipline, and resolve demonstrated they were good men worth following. They were men who lived their talk. They expected their team members to do the same.

When Dianne and I married, we sought churches based principally upon the biblical integrity of the man in the pulpit. It doesn't take long to gauge a pastor by his teaching, by his ability to empower and influence others, and also by the culture within the church. I wanted a pastor I could have a relationship with—one who would speak truth if I had spiritual questions. We found that in Skokie, Illinois, when I attended Northwestern, then later in Dallas, Orlando, and Atlanta.

Here's one of many examples: several months after we moved to Orlando, our house back in Texas was still sitting empty, unsold. Though the mortgage wasn't overwhelming, the burden of a house a thousand miles away weighed heavily. I shared my concern with our Orlando pastor, Bill Sutton, perhaps hoping for some sympathy. He offered an unexpected response.

"That's not your house," he said. "You and Dianne were stewards of a home that God gave you for a season. So it's His to sell, not yours. You should just thank Him in advance for selling it."

I nodded in agreement, but to be honest, I thought Bill was seriously thinking outside the box. God wasn't mailing a mortgage check back to the bank every month. We were. Or was He?

Later, however, as I thought about what Bill had said, I realized he had spoken truth. If I was going to trust God in all aspects of my life, then I would trust Him to bring a buyer. I prayed as Bill suggested, thanking God for selling our (His) house, and it made perfect sense. And He did, in fact, bring a buyer less than thirty days after that conversation—on July 4th, Independence Day!

Destination Marketing at Six Flags

The Great American Scream Machine, an iconic roller coaster that influenced American amusement parks for a generation, re-energized the brand as well as sagging attendance at Six Flags Over Georgia. And it almost didn't happen.

As the 1964 New York World's Fair took shape, President Lyndon Johnson and Texas Governor John Connally looked to the successful Six Flags Over Texas for help and asked Six Flags founder Angus Wynne to oversee the Texas pavilions. Wynne sent Errol McKoy to oversee the entire Lake Amusement Area, and, while there, McKoy visited Coney Island. He was impressed by the historic and fast wooden roller coaster, the Cyclone.

In 1969, after Wynne had made him general manager of Six Flags Over Georgia (at the age of twenty-six!), McKoy suggested that they build a gigantic wooden roller coaster. Wynne responded, "Young man, if you ever do anything that harkens back to the past, you'll have a very short career in theme parks."[5]

After Wynne left the company in 1972, McKoy tried again. This time the reception was much friendlier, and in 1973 the world's tallest, longest, fastest wooden roller coaster opened in Georgia. That season, attendance increased by 350,000 people, and the Scream Machine started a coaster war of sorts, as amusement parks around the country took notice.

In 1977, while I was still working at Stars Hall of Fame, I got a call from Spurgeon Richardson, director of marketing at Six Flags Over Georgia. He needed a sales and promotions manager. My name had been floated as a candidate by someone in the Six Flags organization. I jumped at the chance to interview and was blessed to join Spurge's team within weeks.

For two years, my role as sales and promotions manager at Six Flags mirrored my responsibilities at Seven Seas and Stars Hall of

Fame. We were preselling tickets for corporate outings and youth groups, scheduling concerts and other special events, and connecting with conventions.

Like the last two Six Flags stops and Texas Instruments before that, we relied on segmented direct mail and direct marketing through trade publications to reach schools and colleges, fraternities and sororities, band directors, and church choir and youth directors. We were preselling groups through direct mail while also creating events that would appeal to unique audiences. And we had a great sales staff calling on southeastern companies about corporate outings and the Funseekers Club. We booked jazz bands, Christian talent, and created a marching band competition. The first Christian concert series, featuring emerging artists like Amy Grant, was at Six Flags Over Georgia, with forty-five thousand Saturday visitors. Amy was in her early twenties—such a great young talent—and her "production support" was her guitar and a stool. But she packed the Crystal Pistol theater. The other parks followed our lead on that one.

We created a two-ticket option where a visitor could come the day of a special event and have a second ticket to come at another time. Geographically, we reached out hundreds of miles, often in the direction of the Six Flags parks in Texas and Missouri. The three parks roughly formed the points of a triangle with Memphis, Tennessee, near the center. We shared a footprint in Mississippi, Louisiana, western Tennessee, and Arkansas, and in those areas we partnered on marketing opportunities, primarily direct mail, promoting common events at the multiple locations.

All three parks were sharing ideas and benchmarking each other. It was another learning lab for me.

Because Six Flags had a great reputation nationally and regionally, its name opened doors to other highly respected corporations. Spurgeon had introduced me to co-branding initiatives, which allowed us to extend our brand beyond what we could have reached alone. For example, we partnered with Coca-Cola to offer special tickets for guests. Coke printed the offer on the side of cans, so the effect was to saturate the region with millions of impressions and to connect the Six Flags name with an enjoyable experience: drinking a Coke.

Various companies like General Motors and Dell sponsored rides and shows. One of the more memorable ones was the Chevy Show, where visitors sat in reclining chairs and watched a film projected onto the inside of a dome. Decades before virtual reality or GoPro was a thing, the Chevy Show took viewers inside Corvettes, race cars, airplanes, and boats for a first-person perspective. If you watched the guests inside the show, you could see them lean into a turn or hop in their seats when they hit a bump—even though the seats never moved. A sign outside the show reminded guests of the possibility of motion sickness. (Ironically, I currently live on a road in Atlanta where a portion of the film was shot.)

We worked with many of those same corporations to create events and ticket offers that they marketed for us as an extension of their in-park activities. They sponsored concerts and special events, which were all considered presold or promotion sales. That combination of sales and presold sales generated roughly six hundred thousand of our attendance in 1977. In 1978, my first full season at Six Flags, the park introduced the Mind Bender, the world's first triple-loop steel roller coaster. We grew our presold sales to 1 million tickets, which contributed to our hitting a record of 2.8 million visitors. The park had never done more than 2.4 million. "2.8 in '78!" had been Spurge's vision cry, and we were blessed to reach it.

That's when I crossed paths for the first time with the growing leader of chicken sandwiches. The head of our sponsorship group wanted to make a pitch to a small, regional restaurant company called Chick-fil-A. I didn't know much about the chain other than that they were in malls, served a unique, quality product, and were mostly in six or seven southeastern states. What better place to build a brand and trial than a place with 2.8 million people coming through in a season, primarily from the southeast?

"Go for it," I said. "But you've got to be specific. Pitch a location, a design, and be clear about what's in it for them." In turn, Six Flags had to retain a portion of sales for sponsorship rights.

We met with Jimmy Collins, senior vice president; Bureon Ledbetter, who was general counsel; and Don Millard, their chief financial officer, and pitched them on building a park restaurant. Over the course of multiple conversations, we got to a store design, location, and a pro forma.

The pro forma, I believe, is what soured them on the deal. Six Flags would receive forty percent of revenues, which represented the sponsorship fee and covered the expected decline of our normal fried chicken sales. In other words, Chick-fil-A would not make much, but they could potentially break even while they built their brand through trial and the personal connection with customers who were part of the Six Flags experience. Jimmy, to his credit, wanted to make money, so they chose not to do the deal. We shook hands and parted on good terms, thankful to have made the connection.

"Out of Sight, Out of Mind, Out of Business"

After that season, Errol McKoy, who was by then the executive vice president of SFOG, told us he had been called back to Dallas, where he would serve as president of the Texas State Fair. Spurgeon Richardson was named general manager of Six Flags Over Georgia, giving us a marketing veteran running the park. I was twenty-eight years old, yet Spurgeon was gracious to give me the opportunity to replace him as director of marketing.

As part of the transition, Spurge and I wanted to better understand the "walk-up" part of the business—the people who drove in and bought full-priced tickets. What compelled someone to come up and pay full price . . . and feel good about it? This was a significant challenge in the theme park business: full-price ticket sales. (Sound anything like fast food?)

I was in the park almost every day, sometimes seven days a week, observing how people were taking in the experience. For two years my team and I had been helping large groups of people make plans for future trips to Six Flags. We had grown corporate outings, concerts, and events that had invigorated presales. But the most profitable ticket we could sell was a family stepping up to the front gate. For the park to continue growing at a healthy pace, we needed to create compelling reasons for people to come *today*. If you put an umbrella over everything we were doing in our marketing group, that was the theme. "Why do I need to come to Six Flags today?"

Spurge had a simple phrase he repeated a thousand times: "Out of sight, out of mind, out of business."

Our marketing group's job was to create that truth in the inverse: "In sight, in mind, in business." We needed to create top-of-mind awareness for the park by raising visibility and giving families compelling reasons to remember that Six Flags is relevant to their life and family *today*.

We believed our main gate sales would respond to this question: "What is the compelling, everyday brand promise?" The answer to that question became our challenge and our ad agency's challenge. We needed to do more than talk about the new rides, updated shows, and events.

"Give visibility to the park's features," I said, "but we have to have a brand promise bigger than rides and shows."

This was the beginning of my education in using research and listening to customers to build a brand.

With the help of our advertising agency, McCann Erickson–Atlanta, and custom research, we started to understand guests' emotional engagement with the park. Going to Six Flags was a big family expense, and the research told us people were not buying just the fun-and-functional performance of the Scream Machine or the Mind Bender or the Crystal Pistol shows. Families were attracted for many of the same reasons they were attracted to Disney—the emotional experience and the relational time and engagement with their family, particularly with their children.

That knowledge became a powerful insight for us. With it, we gave McCann new direction. Show the rides and shows, especially the new ones, and the calendar of concerts and special events. But particularly during vacation windows, identify the brand promise for the family—their unique family time at Six Flags.

The gifted Clisby Clarke, a hall-of-fame advertising talent at McCann–Atlanta, took the challenge. Clisby played piano by ear and was a huge Georgia Bulldogs fan (I didn't hold that against him). In fact, that same year he wrote a new fight song, "Bulldog Bite," for the Georgia athletic department. He and his team responded to our challenge with a powerful theme: "Hug Your Kids the Six Flags Way."

It was brilliant. In a single line, they identified the emotional promise, which we could build on with images and in-park experiences. He even wrote music for it. We produced radio and television spots that captured family engagement at Six Flags. They showed the park's brand assets alongside images depicting the relational reward of being with your children and hugging them the Six Flags way.

The campaign was a huge success. Our research confirmed that people immediately identified with it and liked it. The next year, the campaign migrated to some of the other Six Flags parks. It was my first experience with a campaign genuinely capturing what a brand represented. Rewarding, indeed!

The irony for the Robinson family, however, was that I was spending most of my waking hours bringing families together for a wonderful time instead of having a wonderful time with my own family. Our son, Josh, was born in 1979, when Joy was four and a half. On Joy's birthday, we had an event at the park, and I absolutely couldn't get home. Dianne was wonderfully patient; she understood.

We decided she would bring Joy to the park to be with me on her birthday. *This will be great*, I thought. We had in-park characters, so I planned to invite one of them to the party. I got a cake and had it all ready. Then Dianne showed up with little Joy, and when Joy saw that cartoon character in real life, she was scared to death. Dad's best-laid plans . . .

I missed special events like birthdays, but I also missed too many Sundays. I couldn't worship with my family. I couldn't eat dinner with them. Too many nights I came home late. The theme park business is relentless, particularly if your department is responsible for major events.

While I was focused on getting other families into Six Flags based on our brand promise, Spurgeon Richardson was focused on how we delivered on that promise. Spurge insisted the brand promise was much more than just rides and operations and safety. It was also about the interaction and the guest experience. We needed to ramp up the quality of talent we were hiring in the park and improve hospitality training. Thanks to Spurge's influence and our park's leadership team, we succeeded. The result: walk-up attendance went up significantly the first year of the campaign.

Then three and a half years into this ride (pun intended), my phone rang.

THREE

"Test Me"

I was thirty years old in the summer of 1980 when our pastor, Dr. Clark Hutchinson, asked me to lead a $2.5 million fundraising program to build a new educational building for our church and school, which our kids attended. I had no problem with the idea of raising money. Not only would it benefit my kids, but the asset would work six days out of the week instead of Sunday only.

I had never led a fundraising campaign, but I clearly knew it would require our own financial commitment. And though I was in my fourth year as director of marketing for Six Flags Over Georgia, I wasn't making a lot of money. Dianne and I prayed about it, and I agreed to do it. I didn't realize it at the time, but I was on the threshold of a major turning point in my life. You see, I didn't yet understand what *real* giving was all about.

At the first committee meeting, Clark unpacked Malachi 3:10–12 (NIV):

> "Bring the whole tithe into the storehouse, that there may be food in my house. Test me in this," says the LORD Almighty, "and see

> if I will not throw open the floodgates of heaven and pour out so much blessing that there will not be room enough to store it. I will prevent pests from devouring your crops, and the vines in your fields will not drop their fruit before it is ripe," says the LORD Almighty. "Then all the nations will call you blessed, for yours will be a delightful land," says the LORD Almighty.

Clark made the point: "You need to understand. This is the only place in Scripture where God uses the words *test me* and the outcome is positive." And he reminded us that Christ said He came to fulfill the Scriptures, not destroy them.

I did my own study and confirmed this "test me" promise. This was important because there were few things in our marriage on which Dianne and I did not see eye to eye, but the area of giving was one of them. It was not my nature to be a big giver. To put it bluntly, I had pretty tight fists. She had been raised in a home where her father had a giving heart. I had not been raised in a home that tithed. We gave, but not liberally and not systematically. It wasn't something my parents talked about, so I had little biblical perspective about giving.

Because of my commitment to Clark to lead this campaign, however, I couldn't do the job with integrity if I didn't believe and support his message on this biblical principle. This was a faith issue for me, not a money issue.

Totally independent of Dianne, I decided to believe what God said: "Test me on this." The promise is positive. Dianne and I agreed to tithe, and we set an additional amount apart above the tithe toward the campaign. Then we turned in the commitment card, because campaign leadership needed to be among the first to make a commitment.

We started the campaign within the church, but I did not have peace about our financial commitment. When I lay in bed at night or when I prayed as I drove to work, I had no peace over our decision.

Not a good sign! In fact, another number kept coming to mind, and it was more than double the number we had turned in.

My mind was racing . . . there was no way we could afford to give that much. Over and over I calculated my salary and my potential bonus, and the math never worked. It made me break out in a cold sweat.

Finally, one night two weeks after turning in our commitment, we were lying in bed with the lights out, and I knew I had to talk to Dianne about it. "I don't have any peace about this commitment we turned in," I said. "I'm feeling really impressed to change it from *X* to *Y*." I figured that I had surprised her, because it was *more*, not *less*.

There was a quiet pause, then she laughed. *What's on her mind?* She turned on the light and pulled her Bible from the bedside table. She opened it to Psalm 81:10: "Open your mouth wide and see if I won't fill it" (TLB). Next to the verse she had written a number, a weekly amount that, when multiplied by fifty-two weeks and three years (the campaign time frame) was within hundreds of the number God had given me. We both laughed, and cried, and turned off the lights.

The next Sunday we changed the pledge to that amount, and finally I was at peace. But I still wasn't sure how we would make it work financially. Yet I soon learned that was the point: we wouldn't. I didn't know it yet, but God had used Clark and Malachi to change my life.

A Thorough Hiring Process at Chick-fil-A

Two days later I got an unexpected call from Jimmy Collins, Chick-fil-A's chief operating officer. He started the conversation with, "As you may know, we don't have a marketing department at Chick-fil-A."

And I was thinking, *Oh, I knew that. If you had a marketing department, you would have done that in-park deal with me!*

"We have a couple of people trying to do marketing," he continued, "but they really don't have a marketing background. We just don't have what Operators need to help them build their sales. And our same-store sales are slowing down."

He never used the word *brand*. It was a matter of resourcing Operators to build sales. Simple enough, right?

He continued, "Would you have any interest in talking to us? I know you've got a great job and probably love what you do."

"Yes," I said, "that's correct." But I was thinking, *I would absolutely love to talk to you*. Because at that point I had eight years of professional experience with Texas Instruments and Six Flags. I had seen the short-term, transactional focus at TI that undermined the building of a brand around handheld technology (and we see who dominates that market forty years later). And for four years I had watched Six Flags grow, but it was now led by a holding company emerging from bankruptcy, a company that was all about cash. The pressure for quarterly cash performance pinched our capital improvements in the park. Our marketing budget was not growing. We were "milking" the brand, not improving the guest experience and thus the brand.

All the while, I was also thinking back to my pastor's message and wondering, *What's going on here? Is God in this?* I hadn't talked to these folks at Chick-fil-A in over a year and a half. Why was Jimmy calling me now?

"Yes," I said again. "I would be interested in talking with you."

So we made arrangements, and I started the interview process assuming that after a couple of weeks we would know one way or the other. After all, I had interviewed with and gotten my first Six Flags job with one day of interviews.

Wrong! Five and a half months later, I had spent time with

Truett, Jimmy, Dan Cathy, Bubba Cathy, the HR director, the operations director, and anybody who was anybody in the home office, plus a couple of Operators.

The breakneck development of shopping malls across the country was opening huge opportunities for Chick-fil-A to grow with them. Over a two-year period in 1980 and 1981, the chain would add more than one hundred locations, doubling the number of restaurants. The growth rate made Truett more than a bit uncomfortable, but now was the time to put a stake in the ground in these new malls or lose them.

"I don't know how they've been researching me," I told Dianne, "but they're sure thorough." I began to fear that Spurge would find out and tell me, "You know what? If you don't like your job here . . ."

Finally in December 1980, I was having lunch with Truett in his office. They still hadn't made an offer. We were about an hour into the conversation, and I said, "Truett, I really think you've got the makings of a great brand here."

"What do you mean by that?" he asked.

My eye was drawn to the Bible verse he had on a plaque on his desk: "A good name is to be chosen rather than great riches, loving favor rather than silver and gold" (Proverbs 22:1 NKJV).

"It's like the verse there," I said. "A great brand is a great reputation."

Then I said, "We've been talking a long time and I'm a little concerned. I'm doing this all stealth and it's starting to get uncomfortable. Truett, what are you looking for in the ideal marketing candidate? And, am I the guy?"

He put his sandwich down and said, "I have absolutely no idea. All I know is that whatever it is, I don't want to do it." He wasn't smiling. He was dead serious. I was shocked. Then he said, "But this is what I do know: I want to know that you and I can work together until one of us dies. And I intend to outlive you." This time he was smiling. But clearly, he was *not* looking at this as a short-term decision. (This conversation would become huge in helping me to understand what Chick-fil-A was really about.)

"And I want to know we can trust each other and have fun together, but I'll trust Jimmy and the others to figure out if you can do the work. If they think you can do the work, then you may very well be the right candidate. But I'm not prepared to tell you that today.

"The most important decision we make here," he continued, "is who we invite to join the business. Because if you join Chick-fil-A, my goal and expectation is you will never leave here. I'll have another conversation with Jimmy, and we'll let you know, but that's what I'm looking for."

Maybe you've had an interview like that, but not me. I didn't know what to say.

Every other interview I had ever participated in was predominantly about competency and skill set. I had never seen someone so preoccupied with who I was in terms of character and personal chemistry. In effect, he said he was more interested in who I *was* than what I could *do.* And suggesting this would be the only place I would work? Are you kidding me? I'd already had four jobs since grad school.

And yet, I liked everything I had seen about this company: private ownership, the values, Truett's entrepreneurial spirit, the menu. I loved the sandwich, but I wasn't drawn to a career change because of a piece of chicken between two pieces of white bread. I was drawn to this man, the Operator deal he had created, and the chain's unique niche in the malls. Most of all, I liked the idea of coming in on the ground floor. I wouldn't inherit somebody else's marketing plan or organization.

This was the day of the "Uncola" 7UP campaign. I told Dianne, "This is the unburger, and it could be something big." That's what kept my interest in the months-long conversation with Truett when I already had one of the greatest jobs in Atlanta.

"Okay," I told him, "so what's the next step?"

"I'll consult with Jimmy and any others he wants to involve, and we'll decide whether you're the guy or not," he said. "I would think within two or three weeks we'll be able to give you an answer."

My heart sank. "Another two or three weeks . . ."

After months of interviews, I knew my way to the front door. I slowed at Jimmy's office, and he invited me in and asked how the visit had gone. I gave him a flyby of the conversation, and I asked, "What do you think your timing is?" I was hoping for a better answer than I had heard from Truett. The holidays were coming up, and I was ready to settle this one way or the other.

"That's about right," he said. "Probably another couple of weeks. I'll visit with Truett, and I'm probably going to want to have another sit-down with you."

Sure enough, the next week Jimmy and his wife, Oleta, invited Dianne and me to dinner at their home. (This session may have been more about getting to know the lady at the side of Steve Robinson.) Toward the end of the evening, I asked Jimmy the same question. I said, "Okay. Am I the guy or not?"

Jimmy was forthright. He said, "I think everybody's getting pretty excited about your candidacy, but I do need to have one last conversation with Truett before we fully commit and I think of giving you an offer."

Finally, a few days later he called me at my office with an offer, and he invited Dianne and me to the Chick-fil-A staff Christmas party at Bubba Cathy's home. I hurried home and told Dianne they had doubled our income, and we laughed and cried together. A *good* cry.

The next day I met with Spurgeon Richardson, with whom I had worked up close and personal at Six Flags. He knew what I valued, starting with my Christian faith, and I greatly valued his influence on my life.

I said, "Spurge, this is really hard, but I've decided to make a change of direction in my career and leave Six Flags. It's an Atlanta company, privately owned, and it's a great values fit for me."

He interrupted me at that point and said, "Chick-fil-A."

"Well, yeah," I said, "but I thought I'd kept it a secret. How did you find out?"

"I didn't," he said. "But it makes complete sense. You think like they think. What's important to them is important to you and vice versa."

Then he graciously complimented me on my work at Six Flags and said, "But you need to do that. Go for it."

I wasn't starting at Chick-fil-A until January 12, after I led Six Flags through the final marketing plan development and my replacement had transitioned into my position. In the meantime, Dianne and I went to the Christmas party at Bubba's house. We arrived a little late, and when we got to the front door, we heard them inside singing carols. Not secular Christmas songs, but carols. To say this was a little different from the staff Christmas party at the Crystal Pistol would be an understatement. Dianne and I were about to experience a major culture change.

Later in the evening there were gifts, including one for Dianne and me.

Uncontested Market Space

In 1981, I was unfamiliar with the term "Blue Ocean Strategy," a marketplace theory whereby a company seeks an uncontested market space (no rough waters from competitors). The book with that title would not be published until twenty-four years later. But it was obvious to me that Truett Cathy had already found an uncontested market space, shopping malls, that allowed Chick-fil-A to grow in size and strength for more than a decade before competitors moved into the same space.

He created the boneless breast of chicken sandwich, which other chains would not attempt to replicate until 1980. (A short-lived copycat "Filet of Chicken" appeared on some restaurant menus as "Chick-fil-A," leading Truett and Jimmy to frequently ask their lawyer to send cease and desist letters.) He also introduced fast-food dining to the shopping mall more than ten years before food courts became a staple part of mall architecture.

On my first day at Chick-fil-A on January 12, 1981, I walked into a carefully curated product culture: in essence, build mall stores, and produce and sell a lot of delicious sandwiches. The chain had been in business for more than a dozen years and had opened 184 stores, and the brand was still known predominately for their unique and high-quality chicken sandwich. Annual sales were a bit more than $100 million. The menu remained almost identical to the first one created in 1967, with the Chick-fil-A sandwich, potato shoestring fries, coleslaw, lemon pie, Coca-Cola products, and fresh-squeezed lemonade. No one had stepped up to challenge them in the marketplace, so they kept their heads down and continued doing what they did best.

The culture of the business and even the way customers talked about Chick-fil-A was sandwich-centric, since the sandwich was easy for customers to buy and carry as they walked around the mall. So the primary focus was selling more sandwiches.

Jimmy Collins was an operational fanatic, and I mean that in the most positive terms. He was all about figuring out how to make the Chick-fil-A restaurant concept a consistent, repeatable operation—every store looking the same, producing the same food, and offering the same level of service, with every Operator doing it Chick-fil-A's way.

"It doesn't cost any more to make a perfect chicken sandwich," he often said, and he expected the same across the entire menu.

He was administratively strong, and he understood the importance of systems, processes, and standards. Interestingly, though, he was not big on rules. He developed procedures to ensure that operations remained consistent but allowed individual Operators flexibility to exercise personal judgment, particularly around their teams and sales building.

That was the power of the Operator agreement, which attracted top-notch entrepreneurial talent. Truett and Jimmy trusted the Operators to make the right decisions day to day.

My $2 Million Mistake

Shortly after I arrived for my first day at Chick-fil-A, Jimmy invited me to the Monday morning devotional, which was optional but really confirmed I was in a different kind of work environment. My office was in a small, windowless trailer connected to the back of the steel office building on Virginia Avenue in Hapeville. As I unpacked, I heard a rooster crow and thought, *Is this a joke?* I'd gone from screams and rumbling roller coasters outside my office to chicken sandwiches and a neighborhood rooster. Nobody suggested the rooster was anything unusual, just a neighbor with chickens.

Jimmy took me downtown to meet with the ad agency. "They're going to present their ideas for future campaigns," he said.

McCann Erickson was the agency, the same company I had worked with at Six Flags, though a different team. And on the Chick-fil-A side, it was Jimmy and the two folks he had mentioned when he first called me. Wonderful, gracious people, but neither had advertising or marketing experience. And when it came to marketing a mall-based fast-food restaurant chain, I didn't know anything either, which I would soon discover.

The agency rep presented several freestanding newspaper inserts with coupons, the same kind of things I had seen from similar chains, and it looked fine to me. They were designed to drive customers to Chick-fil-A. Isn't that what fast-food brands do?

At the same meeting, Dr. Ken Bernhardt from the business school at Georgia State University presented some of the first customer research Chick-fil-A had ever commissioned, research that gave new insight as to how the brand was known and perceived. I took that presentation back to the office and spent most of my first week studying it. It was my first experience with the voice of the Chick-fil-A customer. And unknowingly, I had just met a lifelong friend and professional associate in Ken.

From his findings, I learned that Chick-fil-A, in fact, was not a destination. After all, we were in malls exclusively. Our market was walking past our stores every day. The data showed that more than 75 percent of the people who ate in the mall didn't make the decision to eat until they were in the mall, and unaided awareness of Chick-fil-A was in the single digits. Ours was a captive audience environment, and we had to figure out how to tap into people who were already in that environment—to give them compelling reasons to walk over to our storefront. This insight should have been a "red flag" for me, but the implications did not immediately hit me.

Chick-fil-A had a history of dropping coupons into newspapers by the hundreds of thousands, as if we *were* a destination. Existing customers showed up with them clutched in their hands. Couponing did allow us to introduce our products, generate some awareness, and create short-term increased sales. But at what price? Our customers and Chick-fil-A were becoming hooked on coupons. Like so many other fast-food restaurants with buy-one-get-one offers and discounted "dollar meals," Chick-fil-A had begun to rely on the instant fix.

I learned in that first meeting that our agency was developing a future campaign called "First 'n' Best." In 1980, McDonald's had introduced the McChicken sandwich, and though its sales were so disappointing it disappeared from their stores for several years, fast foods megabrand had awoken and other burger chains were now trying to get into the chicken sandwich business. McCann's solution was to tell the world that the Chick-fil-A Sandwich was not only the original, but it also tasted much better.

We did not have a line item for chain-wide advertising in the corporate budget. Rather, restaurant Operators committed in their franchise agreement to invest up to 3.25 percent of their gross sales to pay for advertising that the home office placed, including the food and paper cost of any offers.

In late 1981, McCann presented creative for a beautiful multipage, four-color "First 'n' Best" newspaper insert with coupons. Jimmy and I liked it, and I suggested, "If we're going to do this, let's go big." I suggested we enhance the offers and media plan. The agency had suggested direct mail. The piece was so good, I suggested that we dramatically increase the exposure by dropping a version into select newspapers.

The piece hit the market, and almost instantly customers showed up in restaurants. Way *too many* customers. The Atlanta newspapers alone had a combined circulation of nearly half a million, and based on previous redemption percentages in all our markets, we thought we would be okay on our 3.25 percent budget.

Almost overnight sales spiked uncontrollably. Food production challenges soared. We had offered free slices of lemon pie, which like everything on the menu, was made by hand. Our poor kitchen staff was overwhelmed! And that was only one of *many* offers.

The restaurants quickly reached the budget cap for costs, but customers were still showing up with coupons for more free food. By the time the offers expired and the dust settled, the chain had given away $2 million worth of food over and above the restaurants' 3.25 percent budget commitment. That unbudgeted $2 million hit the corporate P&L like a sack of bricks, and my name was mud. And in my first year! I wondered if I'd even make it to year two.

My recommendations had lost the equivalent of almost 2 percent of that year's gross sales. I had been too aggressive about things I didn't fully understand.

The kitchen staffs, the Operators, and our accountants were all angry. Two weeks into the campaign, I went to Jimmy and apologized. "If I'd known what I know now, I wouldn't have made those recommendations," I said. "I was too aggressive with insufficient knowledge."

He was incredibly gracious. He said, "You don't have to apologize. I was a part of the decision too. We just invested $2 million in your education. You'll never make that mistake again."

I know Truett must have been as upset as anybody. He had committed $10 million to build a new home office, and borrowing that much money was already weighing heavily on him. My recommendations had added another $2 million to the load. But he never said anything to me. His body language wasn't good, but he never confronted me about it. I suspect Jimmy counseled him, "Extend some grace to Steve on this because I was there and I approved it too." Both men were models of patient leadership and grace.

And Jimmy was right. I would never make that mistake again. If I had anything to do with it, Chick-fil-A was getting out of the coupon business. Between the "First 'n' Best" experience and the mall customer research insights, that was one fast-food paradigm I didn't want associated with Chick-fil-A ever again!

My "education" process had begun dramatically and expensively, and the lessons were clear:

- Coupons and discounts undermine the value of the brand. They scream, "Our products are not worth full price."

- Coupons are a crapshoot. You can't control the outcome, pace, or quantity of results.
- Maybe worst of all, coupons made Chick-fil-A look like all the other fast-food brands. Not good.

In the heat of the disastrous results, it was easy to say, "No more coupons!" But when we made that strategic commitment in a fast-food business that was surrounded by a paradigm of couponing and deals, we created a huge new challenge.

Our entire Operator family had grown to rely on coupons. The home office had built its advertising around coupons. And now this young guy who just about killed the kitchen staffs with one of his first campaigns, which used coupons, is saying, "No more coupons"?

In my mind, I ran imagined conversations over and over.

"What's that all about?" the Operator demands. "I've got to grow my sales."

"Well, you've got to get your sales up another way," I say.

"And what is that other way, Mr. Director of Marketing?"

"I don't know."

We needed a viable, long-term strategic option quickly. We had to come to the table with ideas, programs, and creative support to build sales another way.

At Six Flags, generating new business had been the responsibility of the marketing department. What were we going to do to drive attendance? So I brought that attitude to Chick-fil-A. Quickly, however, I learned that my new job was different—it was to equip the Operators with the tools to generate new business. Sales was not my responsibility; it was theirs. If we hadn't gone through the coupon crisis, I might have worked for years before coming to that realization. That event was a shock treatment.

Operators are the marketing agents of the Chick-fil-A brand.

They will naturally control the ebb and flow of a marketing investment to maximize the realities of their growth and income goals. Our job as a marketing group was to equip them to grow the business—both the profits and the brand—as fast as they wanted to grow it in a healthy way.

Our strategic option was standing in front of us. Truett Cathy had built his business at the Dwarf House through personal relationships with customers, not coupons. His experience would become our model for growing Chick-fil-A.

The "First 'n' Best" coupon disaster led us to determine we would *not* be a transaction-chasing brand. We would build Chick-fil-A through personal relationships. We didn't know fully how that would look or what tools we might offer, but we knew there was no personal relationship in a coupon. A customer found it in the newspaper or the mailbox, cut it out, and traded it in for food. And in the process, Chick-fil-A looked like any other fast-food brand.

But we knew that Chick-fil-A was not just another fast-food brand. We needed to figure out how to market it so *that* reality came through loud and clear. The journey would take us to a new Blue Ocean–style uncontested market space.

Selecting a Staff

We needed to build a marketing staff, beginning with somebody to join me in the field to listen to Operators and learn the business from their side. I had a clear idea where to start. David Salyers had worked at Six Flags the summer after he graduated from high school, running the Dahlonega Mine Train. Then for three summers while he attended the University of Georgia, he worked as our public relations intern. David helped with publicity events, press tours, and concerts.

Although I knew David well, I still did not want to hire him without engaging in the appropriate process. As Truett had told me, the most important decision you make is who to invite into the business. He was relying on me to make wise hiring choices, and he was also very active in the process. For years he had interviewed every Operator candidate and every staff candidate because as far as he was concerned, if you were going to become a part of Chick-fil-A, you would never go anywhere else. So every selection needed to be a wise one. He and Jimmy had spent more than five months interviewing me before making an offer, and through that process I came to understand that they were looking for competency, character, and chemistry in the people. Throughout my Chick-fil-A career, I would attempt to apply those criteria.

First, competency. I learned to be less concerned about the specific skill set that somebody brought to the table. Instead, I evaluated whether they had the ability and desire to be a learner. At Chick-fil-A, as at most growing organizations, we wanted people who could do more than one or two things. We wanted them to demonstrate the ability to learn new skills through their personal entrepreneurship, as well as show a willingness to take on new challenges and opportunities.

People ask, "Do grades matter?" Yes, they matter because grades demonstrate to some degree whether the person is a good learner. Have they demonstrated a listening, learning attitude? My first test was not just the skill set a person had, but his or her history of learning, at school and in other jobs.

Second, character. Would this person thrive in the Chick-fil-A culture? Was there such personal alignment with the Corporate Purpose and the underlying values that they would thrive in that environment? Also, would I want my children working for this person? If the answers were yes, then the person was probably a viable candidate.

Third, chemistry. Had this person demonstrated—and could I see this person generating—followership completely independent of title? This person should be able to cast vision as well as demonstrate great listening and great processing on his or her feet. And because this person was a great listener and had intellectual capacity, then when she did open her mouth (or he opened his), this person added value to the project or the conversation. People would naturally gravitate to this person, no matter what his or her title might be.

David Salyers fit every category. And as it turned out, he knew more about Chick-fil-A than I had imagined. When Truett was speaking to students at the University of Georgia, the two of them had met. Truett was so impressed, he invited David to the Chick-fil-A Operator Seminar—my first seminar. In fact, to my surprise, I checked him in at our registration table. Truett and I both recruited him, and David agreed to come aboard.

Right away, we dove into Ken Bernhardt's research and made numerous store visits. It was clear that the mall was not just a place to do business. The mall was our primary medium. Not coupons. Not paid media. And because we were paying high-priced rent to be in the mall, we had to make it work for us. Up to that point, the only tools Operators had were Be Our Guest cards and standing out on the lease line sampling chicken on toothpicks. Those were powerful tools—good food and personal connections.

David and I traveled from store to store, mall to mall, discovering what Operators needed to build their business. We weren't thinking of building a brand then. We were just building business, building sales profitably.

The best Operators were already figuring out how to use their lease line and the mall environment to gain product trial and awareness. So we built the initial mall-based marketing plan literally from the menu board out, redesigning it to work harder from farther away.

We designed new point-of-sale materials to work on the store counters and at the lease line. We designed materials to help support sampling chicken, lemonade, and lemon pie. We created cross promotions with other mall tenants to take advantage of their customer bases, and we designed in-mall billboards.

During those restaurant visits we discovered the power of the Operator concept by simply getting to know them. They weren't managers. They were legitimate business entrepreneur leaders. They were smart, and they had opinions of their own. They weren't punching the clock forty hours a week. They were doing whatever it took to grow the business profitably and take care of the customer. And they weren't afraid to tell us what we were doing well or what we were *not* doing well to support them. They respected the partnership with Chick-fil-A, but they had no problem leaning into our responsibility to help them grow their business.

Some of our most important product introductions originated with Operators. In 1982, Dr. Bill Baran joined Chick-fil-A as our nutrition and new product expert. Like David and me, he spent part of his time visiting Operators. Returning from a trip to Richmond and Virginia Beach, he told us that an Operator up there (Red Witten) had seen parents taking chicken out of the bun and cutting it into smaller pieces for their children. Red began experimenting, slicing smaller pieces before cooking, and even had a local metal shop create a basket specifically designed to fry these "nuggets."

Bill said kids as well as adults were begging for the product, and he believed we might have a winner. He contacted our chicken suppliers and asked them to develop a technique for cutting breast meat into half-ounce pieces, and he asked our equipment manufacturers to create the right cooking basket. Soon we had several restaurants running trials on "Chick-fil-A Nuggets," using the same recipe as the sandwich. Customers loved them.

At the same time, our team had developed a recipe using a pressure cooker for chicken noodle soup made from scratch in restaurants. Once again, we ran in-store trials, and we were confident that both products, which we planned to introduce in 1983, would succeed.

FOUR

Purpose

Why We Exist

In the early 1980s, Truett and Jimmy established the executive committee, with Dan and Bubba and the top officers from finance, design and construction, real estate/legal, marketing, and operations. At one of our first meetings, Buck McCabe, chief financial officer, distributed the corporate financials. Though we had discussed sales and expense numbers before, this was the first time I had seen the entire report. Buck guided us through the report, explaining key points.

My eyes landed on a line that showed Chick-fil-A's charitable giving, and it was about 10 percent of the corporate profits. Truett was tithing corporate profits! As sole owner of Chick-fil-A, he might have directed that portion of income to his personal bank account or reinvested it in the company. But he believed Chick-fil-A was God's company, and Truett saw himself as a steward of the asset more than an owner.

That moment early in my Chick-fil-A career became a huge encouragement to me. I was coming to understand the promises of Malachi 3 around tithes and offerings, and implicitly embedded in that is how we view money and our stewardship responsibility. In this incredible and faith-based promise, God says that if we will follow this principle of tithing, honoring, and worshiping Him, He will bless us. He does not describe what those blessings will be. He does not say we'll never have problems. He just says, "I will bless you." He says, "I will protect you from the devourer. I will protect your crops. I will protect your fields." What does that mean? I took it to mean exactly what it says. He doesn't promise prosperity, but rather blessing and protection when we are faithful.

Reflecting on the long-term success at Chick-fil-A, let me state with no false humility: we were not that smart. And, quite frankly, other Chick-fil-A executive committee members would also say we weren't smart enough individually or collectively to explain the success of Chick-fil-A.

We had a founder and CEO whom the world would not consider particularly educated (he never attended college). Truett had a speech impediment when he was younger, but he overcame it so that now, when he spoke, people listened. He was one of the wisest people I have ever met. Truett Cathy applied what he knew to be biblical and Christian principles in his life and in his business. Within months of my joining the company, I had already seen numerous examples. Then I saw that line on the financials, showing that he was applying one of the most challenging principles to his business. During the course of my thirty-four years at Chick-fil-A, I saw a man in a prayerful, humble, obedient, servant relationship with God, and I saw that same man lead a company of men and women to heights the world marveled at. He created a simple product—boneless breast of chicken between two pieces of white bread with two pickles—that the world fell in love with.

Watching him interact with thousands of people over the years, I saw him respect the dignity of every person. He tried to see every person as God sees us. This is biblical, ground-level principle one, and business principle one as well. The Bible says that in the beginning we were created in God's image (Genesis 1:26). We have a soul, a spirit, and a personality. Truett believed that truth and taught it by his example. I suspect as a boy he watched his mother as she ran the family's boarding house and treated everyone with dignity—not just as a renter, but as someone to serve.

The Bible also says we were created "a little lower than the angels" (Hebrews 2:7 NKJV). We were created to lead and have dominion over creation. God put creation in our hands. That is stewardship. I came to understand that everything we enjoy, everything we touch and have in our hands, including relationships, money, and talent, we have a stewardship accountability for.

I share this from a position of honor, and I marvel at how God favored Truett and Chick-fil-A. When Truett had something important to say, God gave him the words to say it in an impactful and usually simple and clear way. He modeled for all of us how to apply smart business principles, which he did not see in conflict with biblical principles. Neither do I. And when we applied them, things worked, and in many cases they worked exceptionally well.

Truett created a business that reflected who he was as he tried to live out what the apostle Paul challenged us to do—live in the image of Christ.

I don't know if Truett intended to demonstrate stewardship to the executive committee through tithing the business, but he did to me. I thought about it many times over the decades as we made decisions.

Crisis Clarifies Purpose

In the early 1980s, the global economy faced a significant recession. In the United States, unemployment and interest rates skyrocketed, and retail sales were in a tailspin. Chick-fil-A was not immune to its devastating effects. In 1981, the company saw same-store sales drop for the first time in its history, and this continued into 1982. Shopping malls, the exclusive location of Chick-fil-A restaurants, had stopped coming out of the ground, halting new store growth. Worse, the capital and financing costs of having opened stores in more than a hundred malls in two years weighed on the corporate profits, as did the $10 million note for the new home office. And don't forget the $2 million "First 'n' Best" debacle.

Truett called his executive team together and asked us, "What are you going to do about it?"

In the current mall and retail sales environment, we had no quick answer. So we scheduled a two-day retreat at nearby Lake Lanier Lodge for the executive committee to discuss with Truett his question and our options. In that small room with Truett were Jimmy Collins, Dan Cathy, Bubba Cathy, Bureon Ledbetter, Buck McCabe, Don Millard, Perry Ragsdale (who led design and construction), and me. For the better part of the first day, we reviewed our plans and our finances, confident that per-store sales would respond to the new nugget and soup products.

Those hundred new stores we had opened in 1980 and 1981 had been a drag in the early months of their operation because Chick-fil-A was still a new idea. In 1982, those hundred stores had just begun to grow their customer base and their sales. We were opening only eighteen new restaurants in 1982.

From a marketing standpoint, we had developed strategies to highlight our new products, with tools to maximize sampling and Be Our Guest cards offering free nuggets or soup. We planned extensive in-mall giveaways; nuggets were easy to sample at the lease line and also take around and share in mall offices. A great new finger-food entrée was ready to go.

Given the financial pressures, though, we had cut headquarters' marketing expenses severely, so we couldn't financially supplement advertising that the Operators might be planning. Once again, however, the key to building the Chick-fil-A brand resided with the Operators, not the corporate marketing department. Operators were appropriately becoming the primary marketing agents of the business, and that process was accelerated, in part out of the financial reality that we didn't have any cash lying around to supplement their spending.

I believe crisis does more than reveal and shape character—it is also a primary catalyst of learning and creativity. Human nature drives us to be more proactive, sensitive learners when we're in a crisis. We're more receptive to the counsel of others.

The sun rose on the second day of our retreat, and we came together again. We agreed, based on day one, that our 1983 plans looked good. Dan Cathy changed the subject and suggested we look deeper than new products, financials, and plans. "Why are we in business?" he asked. "Why are we here?" He noted, and the rest of us agreed, that folks at Chick-fil-A were concerned, maybe even a little afraid. They had hitched their futures to Chick-fil-A. How did leadership see the future? What were our plans? Did we need to be really clear about why we were in business—what's *really* important—in good times or bad?

What was the purpose of our existence? To push more and more chicken sandwiches across the counter? No. Serving chicken sandwiches quickly was not the reason Chick-fil-A existed; that was never how Truett Cathy saw Chick-fil-A. But neither he nor any of us had crystallized in words why Chick-fil-A *did* exist. We all embraced Truett's values, and they were embedded in the culture. But now it was time to put our "why" into words. Everyone at Chick-fil-A needed to know. That became our day two assignment.

Our "purpose" model, as I just noted, was Truett, who, at sixty-one, could have retired and turned over his 255 Chick-fil-A restaurants to Dan and Bubba and lived off the income stream for the rest of his life. Or he could have sold the business. But he still had things to do. Like his wife, Jeannette, had told him twenty years earlier when he had his cancer scare: "God isn't finished with your life yet."

All for God

Since 1946, at the end of their first week operating the Dwarf Grill (later Dwarf House), Truett and his brother Ben had closed the restaurant on Sunday. Truett maintained that closed-on-Sunday policy with the founding of Chick-fil-A, and he often said it was the best business decision he ever made. He closed his restaurants on Sunday to honor God. He also tithed the company's profits to honor God. He had taught Sunday school lessons to thirteen-year-old boys since 1951 to honor God and give his team a day of rest. But these things were just the outward signs of a heart truly devoted to the God he loved. Truett didn't live this life and honor God out of a sense of duty but out of loving desire. He *wanted* to do these things. And he had nailed down these nonnegotiables long before Chick-fil-A took off.

As we attempted to answer Dan's question, "Why are we in business?" we were trying to put into writing the way Truett had been living out his business practices and his life—the way he had already been leading us.

So the first phrase of our answer became "To glorify God"—that is, to give God glory and reverence because He created us, loves us, and is the source of everything in this world, including all that we have and enjoy. The Ten Commandments begin with God. The most ancient Old Testament scripture states, "Love the Lord your God with all your heart and with all your soul and with all your strength" (Deuteronomy 6:5 NIV). And Jesus acknowledged this as the greatest commandment (Mark 12:29–30).

But how does one glorify God? Looking again to Truett for guidance, we realized he saw everything that he owned, whether possessions or relationships, as a gift from God and thus belonging to God. So if God owns everything, then Truett was simply a caretaker. A steward, looking after God's possessions that He had put temporarily into Truett's and our hands. Therefore, "we glorify God *by* being faithful stewards of all that God has entrusted to us." Nothing in the statement we were crafting was more important to Truett than that phrase "by being faithful stewards." The most important word in that phrase was *by*, just two letters. His premise was this business does not glorify God unless it is built upon great stewardship of the assets, talents, influence, and relationships entrusted to us. He felt accountability to his Creator—accountability for everything the Creator put into his hands and, thus, our hands—so he wanted a business that focused on doing those things well.

Then there is the second phrase in the greatest commandment, "Love your neighbor as yourself." With that command, I am again reminded of Truett, one of the most loving, generous men I have ever known. Bestselling author Ken Blanchard wrote a book called *The Generosity Factor* based on Truett's life, saying he had never known a more generous person.

Why are we in business? In part, "to have a positive influence on all who come in contact with Chick-fil-A," a statement that is completely consistent with Truett's attitude toward the business. Operators throughout the chain hire thousands of young people every year to work in Chick-fil-A restaurants, and for many of those young people it's their first job. Imagine the influence Operators have by creating a safe, positive, loving work environment. Then their team members extend that love into the dining room and take it home to their families and into their schools, creating a positive influence wherever they go.

By the end of the second day and hours of drafts, debate, and prayer, we had written a purpose statement to express why we exist:

> *To glorify God by being a faithful steward of all that is entrusted to us, and to have a positive influence on all who come in contact with Chick-fil-A.*

The Holy Spirit had orchestrated something we had not even planned to do. We had captured in words how Truett had already been leading the business. We all had been attempting to live his model, and now we had a statement to help us and those who followed us. We were not a "Christian business," but rather a business where the owners and leadership aspired to apply and live out biblical principles.

In 1982, at our moment of deepest financial crisis, we stepped back and determined why Chick-fil-A existed. We embraced that purpose and were sobered by it. We were all a part of leading a unique business, to say the least. For me, I knew without question that I was where God wanted me to be.

Now, how would we unpack this for the staff and Operators? The company appeared to be in crisis. This would be the last thing they would expect to come out of a leadership meeting dedicated to dealing with our financial and sales challenges. We decided to wait—to pray and think about it. When we came back to the issue, we had total consensus to introduce the corporate purpose at the same time we would announce our commitment to our 1983 plans for growth, including new product rollouts. In essence, if Chick-fil-A is God's gift to Truett, then He can choose to bless us going forward or shut us down.

The reaction? Amazing. A peace seemed to fall on the business. Folks loved the purpose statement. They identified with what they already knew: Chick-fil-A was about more than profits. And everybody leaned into their work and trusted God to lead us out of the crisis. Or not. (The staff even gifted a bronze plaque of the purpose statement to Truett later that year. It still sits at the front door of the Chick-fil-A support center.)

Then in 1983, Truett astounded us with a decision that defied logic and yet further revealed his heart for God and for young people. After Truett spoke to a group of business students at Berry College near Rome, Georgia, he and Jeannette toured the campus with the college president, Gloria Shatto. The school had been started in the early twentieth century by Martha Berry, offering education for the first time to poor mountain children. The Berry trustees had recently closed the beautiful Berry Academy high school campus. Truett and Jeannette admired the granite dormitories and classroom buildings in their idyllic wooded setting, thought about the history of the place, and wondered what would become of them. They both had strong feelings while there, and Jeannette even said, "I feel like I'm standing on holy ground."

During a period of a few hours, Truett had a vision for housing students recruited within Chick-fil-A who would live in the former academy dormitories and attend Berry College on scholarships funded by Chick-fil-A and the college. (The plan would later expand to include foster homes for children and a summer camp.)

Truett came to the executive committee and laid out his plan and asked for our advice. He was not asking for a vote or for our approval—this would not be owned or operated by Chick-fil-A, Inc., but rather by a foundation that he and Jeannette would establish and fund.

But consider the ramifications of a commitment of this magnitude, starting with the refurbishing of dorms and a dining hall. Truett and Jeannette envisioned 125 scholarship students living in the dorms. The foster homes and camp would require even more infrastructure and staff. Less than a year earlier, Truett had asked us what we were going to do about the financial crisis we were facing.

He and Jeannette took us all up to Berry, along with his pastor and best friend, Dr. Charles Q. Carter. We were impressed but not convinced. Every member of the executive committee advised against Truett's idea. But Truett and Jeannette believed this was what God was calling them to do. They followed through on all their plans, creating the WinShape Foundation in 1984. The influence of the scholarships, children's homes, and camps exceeded all their expectations. It had unprecedented impact and is still going strong decades later.

Principles of the Chick-fil-A Culture

Some readers may have a difficult time grasping the fundamental principles that underlie Chick-fil-A. They are ones I have learned in my Christian walk and have attempted to apply to my life, as did Truett. We didn't apply those principles perfectly at Chick-fil-A, but when we relied on God's promises, like treating people as we would want to be treated, or honoring the Sabbath, or tithing, or so many others, the mystery of God's favor occurred. His favor seemed to clearly follow our steps of faith.

God favored Truett with wisdom that he developed and exercised by reading his Bible, particularly the book of Proverbs. He relied on that wisdom to select strong, capable leaders in every area of the company. He also relied on that discernment in selecting every restaurant Operator in the early years of the chain.

The executive committee individually and collectively sought

God's wisdom and perspective. We prayed for it regularly. We relied on divine insight and the corporate purpose as a filter. We studied other leaders and tried to become leaders who did more than just run a successful business; we wanted to have a positive impact on all those we led and serve in a way that might lead people to ask, "Why is Chick-fil-A so different?"

In the year after we faced major sales declines and established the corporate purpose, same-store sales increased by more than 29 percent over the previous year—including new stores, total sales went up 36 percent. The mall industry had not turned around, but Chick-fil-A had.

In 1983, another tangible picture of an amazing turnaround came when forty-six Operators were given Lincoln Continentals as part of the reward program, Symbol of Success, which Truett had started in the 1970s. It worked like this: Operators who increased their sales by 40 percent in a year would receive the car for a year, and if they repeated a second 40 percent increase, they kept the Lincoln for good. The forty-six cars were parked on the tarmac at Hartsfield International Airport when those Symbol of Success winners returned from the 1984 Operator Seminar in Bermuda.

The Lake Lanier meeting that led to the corporate purpose took my understanding of Truett's perspective about what he owned and didn't own to a whole new level. I had worked at two companies where, like almost all public corporations, leadership acknowledged its accountability to shareholders. They were stewards on behalf of shareholders. And I understood that; I owned stocks.

When I came to Chick-fil-A, I felt a similar responsibility to the single shareholder, Truett.

But what I heard Truett, Dan, and Bubba say to corporate leadership in that meeting was, "You are stewards who are accountable to a much higher level than to us. Chick-fil-A isn't about us. This business and this sandwich are gifts."

Before that meeting and afterward, Truett often said there was nothing complicated about putting a piece of boneless, breaded chicken breast on a buttered bun with two pickles. So the sandwich was a gift, an opportunity to build a business in a space with no comparable competing product. And he rode the wave of mall development, another gift, as we built the business for fifteen years.

With that perspective, when the wave of mall development hit the shore and crashed in 1982, we knew that if Chick-fil-A was not ours, then God must have something else in mind. Our role was to acknowledge and steward God's gift, honor Him, and positively influence others along the way. And to seek His wisdom on the next steps to accomplish this.

FIVE

A New Brand Paradigm

The marketing support at McDonald's, Burger King, Wendy's, or almost any other franchise restaurant brand can be represented by an upside-down pyramid, where most of the control, strategies, and money is controlled at the top by the home office. Those brands rely principally on media and "deals" or price to drive customers to their restaurants, and the local store managers are empowered to do virtually no marketing activity at the store level.

When I joined Chick-fil-A, the company was following a similar model, with each restaurant franchisee sending 3.25 percent of total gross sales to the home office to pay for system-wide marketing and advertising. We were driving transactions from Atlanta, yet as we spent more time in the field with the Operators, the entire marketing team was raising the same question: Why are we trying to build sales out of Atlanta when we have these high-caliber leaders in the restaurants, exclusively in malls?

Even before I arrived at Chick-fil-A, Truett had encouraged Operators to become "the mayor of the mall." If they became the most helpful tenant in the mall, they would build relationships and spread their influence, making a positive influence on people they interacted with. Each of those relationships would lead to new business opportunities.

From a marketing perspective, we were focused on making the mall the medium, starting at the lease line, where we offered samples of food. After all, Operators were paying a premium for the opportunity to market to an audience walking through the malls. Each of those encounters created an additional opportunity to create a first-time trial and a positive encounter with a potential customer. Expanding out, we asked how Operators might work with other merchants. How could they tie in with events in the mall?

We learned from Operators who were doing these things effectively, then we started packaging more and better ways of sampling product at the store, sampling product out in the mall, sampling product at other merchants, creating events with other merchants, and creating events with the mall. Our team created more options for Operators to make the mall the medium, principally using their food and their people. With that mind-set, the Operators innovated even more. When we saw a great idea, we captured it, packaged it, and sent it back out to all the other Operators.

Then we decided to truly flip the industry paradigm on its ear from a marketing point of view, including how it was funded, by putting our money where our "mouth" was. We looked hard at that 3.25 percent accrual for marketing that we were collecting from the Operators and realized that if we wanted to market the business from the restaurant up, we had to remove stumbling blocks. The 3.25 percent was a huge one. Some Operators were saying, "I don't have any money to spend for local marketing" because they were paying the marketing accrual off the top. The accrual also created a counter-productive expectation for Operators that corporate marketing was responsible for driving their sales.

After a few years working with Operators and listening to our department team, I recommended to Truett and Jimmy that we needed to stop charging the accrual. I hated to give up the funding, and I knew the minute we did, we would probably never reinstitute it. But we needed to motivate Operators to spend whatever they required in their stores, and later in their markets, to grow the business and the brand. And if they weren't happy with sales, then they could look only to themselves for answers.

Truett and Jimmy agreed, and we ended the marketing accrual. That happened before we opened our first restaurants outside malls, so we were well-positioned to have Operators as the primary marketing agents on the street as well. We had flipped the traditional marketing paradigm in fast food upside down.

That decision led to another question: Who is going to do that marketing work at the restaurant, and how might Operators best invest the dollars they had been sending to the home office marketing department?

Operators would not have time to manage marketing on top of their other day-to-day responsibilities, and yet they could not afford to let a day go by without someone marketing the restaurant and the brand. A couple of the most successful Operators had dedicated financial resources for store marketing directors, and we began to consider and develop that model. We asked other Operators, "You have shift managers and kitchen managers. Why not have someone whose leadership is dedicated to growing your business every day? Someone who sells the brand and helps build relationships."

David Salyers often asked, "Mr. or Ms. Operator, who is building your sales for you every day?"

Operators might say they were handling marketing, but the reality was that they had so much going on, they couldn't possibly work on growing the business every day.

Every day was key. A restaurant's marketing director could not succeed if he or she got pulled behind the counter to help serve the lunchtime rush. Marketing a single Chick-fil-A restaurant, which was a potential multimillion-dollar business, deserved a full-time position.

So to create momentum for restaurant-based marketing, we introduced the Unit Marketing Director concept (UMD), which was developed at a meeting among a group of Chick-fil-A Operators and some home office staff at a hotel room in Arlington, Texas. Coming out of this meeting, the staff agreed to create the first-ever training program, and Operators Wayne Hassler, Michael Tucker, and Frankie Turner agreed to dedicate a full-time staff member to marketing. Each of them hired someone who was highly relational—who liked meeting people and had a natural bent to sell. Someone who could communicate and be persuasive and also pay attention to details because they were planning and executing. They did not need to be proficient behind the counter.

Our corporate marketing team communicated closely with the participating Operators and UMDs. As we learned, we developed components of an infrastructure to support them at the corporate marketing level, which included recruiting guidance, training and development tools, and sales and brand-building tools.

At the same time, sales results for those restaurants began to prove the value of a restaurant-based marketing director. They created ideas like Spirit Night, Daddy-Daughter Date Night, and other restaurant events that engaged the community. Other Operators saw their success and joined the movement. Over the course of several years, virtually every Operator would have at least one full-time employee marketing the restaurant. Some now have more, committing to additional marketing staff at certain thresholds, such as each additional million dollars in sales, to maintain sales growth momentum.

So years before Chick-fil-A became a national brand, we had flipped the model for funding and executing marketing upside down. Even now, restaurant Operators and market Operator teams, not the home office, provide 80 to 85 percent of tactical and financial support for execution of brand marketing. We provide them with the tools and training they need, but they finance and participate in the execution.

That model allowed us at the home office to focus on *what only we could do* to create tools and resources that drove emotional connections and brand value. Quite frankly, that's a heck of a lot more fun. Focusing on hospitality is fun. College sport sponsorships and engagement is fun. Paradigm-busting advertising is fun. Store design influence is fun. Applying technology to customer-interfacing experiences is fun. Apparel design is fun. It goes on and on and on.

If we had focused on driving store counts, transaction counts, and quarterly returns, there is no question in my mind that Chick-fil-A would not be what it is today, because we wouldn't have had time or the creative license to help shape a brand that was designed to create emotional connections. What marketing does under a transaction paradigm doesn't look anything like what marketing can do under a scenario of relationship and emotional connections.

Operators took the "mayor of the mall" marketing mentality into their communities when we began opening freestanding restaurants. Truett's advice to become the most helpful tenant in the mall worked just as well outside, as Operators and their marketing directors sought opportunities to serve businesses, schools, houses of faith, and athletic teams in their area. This is the answer to David Salyers's question, "Who is building your sales for you every day?"

Penetration of Chick-fil-A restaurants then grew within certain markets, so Operators began to see the need for a coordinated effort to build the brand in their cities. This birthed the Area Marketing Director concept (AMD). Like their counterparts in the restaurant, AMDs would find and negotiate local promotional partnerships, create charity events, and engage Chick-fil-A restaurants on behalf of the entire city. They wouldn't do much around planning and buying media; the agency would manage that on behalf of the market (with a budget the Operators would approve).

At the home office, we developed training and an annual catalog of materials for UMDs and AMDs to develop plans activating real food, people, Cows, and influence. Our involvement ensured that marketing through the restaurants remained consistent with the way we wanted the brand and sales to be built. We provided templates for planning, scheduling, budgeting, creative, and execution; then they found the opportunities unique to their city or store.

Decades after ending the marketing accrual, we continued to suggest that Operators invest about 3 percent of their sales in marketing their business locally, but we didn't dictate or contractually obligate how much they spent. Even at that level, however, their competition would be significantly outpacing their advertising budgets, often by a factor of two. But when you're building a brand based on emotional engagement rather than transactions, an investment at the personal engagement level is many times more efficient and effective than a media-weighted strategy.

What we did out of Atlanta with media was to provide brand "air cover," while the Operators in their markets ran an effective and consistent ground game. But the ground game came first. If the stores were not creating relationships in their markets, then the limited amount of media support we provided was not going to help.

Story by Story

As noted, we were never going to outspend the competition on advertising. They had millions of dollars for marketing campaigns. We, on the other hand, were committing most of our capital to new stores, thus Operator opportunities, and building the Chick-fil-A brand around our people. Chick-fil-A people became the source of stories—stories that would be passed along and generate buzz for the brand.

The first time we decided to manage and accelerate this process was 1982. We needed a public relations director—the popular phrase today is a "storyteller."

A brand telling its own story is less powerful than when the customers or members of the media family tell those stories. Or put another way, I believed we would never be able to tell stories that genuinely captured the heart and the values of Chick-fil-A through advertising and have them be credible.

Interestingly, Truett wondered what stories we had to tell. He felt we were selling chicken sandwiches, not telling stories. In his humility, he didn't see the value of his own story told with third-party credibility. Over time, I convinced him and Jimmy that to reach the media, we needed a public relations professional who understood media and knew how to deal with editors, writers, and broadcasters—who knew how to position stories and write releases, and how to deal with a crisis if one ever arose. Our job was to equip key constituents—not just media, though certainly they're at the top of the list—to understand the key stories embedded in Chick-fil-A that capture why the brand is unique.

Why are we closed on Sunday? There's a story that goes back to Truett's first restaurant.

How did Truett create this simple sandwich? There's a story.

What's this Operator deal all about? You share half the store profits with them? Another story.

New products, new restaurants, team member scholarships, and major and local sponsored events were all stories, each with a unique meaning for a different audience. Media paid attention to unique material. And remember, there was no social media then.

Truett and Jimmy gave me the go-ahead, and we hired a search firm, who identified a superb candidate in Don Perry at General Electric in Louisville, Kentucky. Don had worked in both the consumer and business-to-business side of GE public relations. He was a Valdosta, Georgia, native and an honor student from the University of Georgia's Grady College of Journalism.

Our interview process with Don did not last as long as mine did—we couldn't keep bringing him down from Kentucky for six months—but he spent significant amounts of time with David Salyers and me, with our human resources director, and with Jimmy. Then he visited with Truett—if this worked, the two of them would be spending a lot of time together—and they hit it off. Like Truett's less-than-prosperous beginnings, Don's rural upbringing in south Georgia was tied to family and hard work, though for him it was in tobacco fields. That became an important connection for the two of them. Don was a man of integrity. He had an impressive résumé. He had good judgment, humor, and deep family values. I had no idea how good a friend he would become to Truett and me.

I also had no idea that his work would help transform Truett into a brand in his own right.

Don began arranging speaking engagements for Truett, and he heard Truett's story over and over. Truett talked about growing up in his mother's boarding house and her total commitment to her boarders. He told of working beside her in the kitchen shelling peas and washing dishes, and that the first time he saw her eyes closed was when she was in her casket. Truett's genuine transparency, his willingness to share his heart, and his ability to engage an audience became the assets Don featured to help establish Truett as the public face of Chick-fil-A.

Truett and Don traveled together often and became trusted friends. Don scheduled select media tours, particularly in new markets where we were trying to grow, with Truett speaking alongside Operators to help build the brand. Don became Truett's PR agent, not just Chick-fil-A's PR agent.

Truett trusted him and empowered him. If Don recommended something, pro or con, Truett listened to him. Don knew how Truett thought and how he wanted to present the business, because he heard him talk about it hundreds of times.

Don believed his job was never about presenting the brand himself; it was about helping Truett to present the brand the way Truett wanted to present it.

The *Atlanta Journal-Constitution* reported in 1986:

> If Truett Cathy wasn't a successful businessman, he could earn a living as a motivational speaker. The Chick-fil-A magnate wowed a group of about 30 at the Southside Public Officials' luncheon last week with his childhood tales of selling Cokes for a profit and delivering papers for *The Atlanta Journal*.
>
> Cathy told the audience that "we gradually become a part of those people we associate with," whether good or bad. And he asked everyone to consider their "power of influence" over other people.[6]

Until the Cows came along, we had one icon in the business, and it was Truett—in large part because of Don's leadership and his personal hands-on management with the media and community relations spaces. In fact, in 1985 Truett received the Atlanta Distinguished

Public Relations Award from the city's chapter of the Public Relations Society of America.

Jimmy Collins, Chick-fil-A's president and COO, was both engaging and charismatic and could have taken a similar role as a spokesman for the chain. But Jimmy believed there should be only one spokesperson for the brand, and that was going to be Truett. That allowed Don to focus all his energy around Truett—how to message with him and how to unpack stories the way Truett could unpack them.

Paradigm Buster: Waffle Fries

Chick-fil-A, and every business for that matter, has three constituents:

Customers
Operators (operations)
Ownership (shareholders)

I believe this priority order is crucial.

If you ever move Operators or ownership ahead of customers, you'll potentially make less than optimal, or even bad, decisions. As long as you keep customers first, the other two will benefit naturally. Operators will win. Ownership will win. But the tension never goes away. Operators want operational ease. They want immediate results. When you're building a brand, you don't always get immediate results. And when you do the things that really make the brand most rewarding, valuable, and endearing, it's not always operationally easy.

Ownership might say, "I want to do this," or, "I think we ought to do that." And because they own the company, they have the right to see it through. But it may not be *best*.

In the early 1980s, Chick-fil-A had been developing new products with a heavy operations focus, which seemed logical. After watching the team work for several years, however, it became increasingly clear that they *were* developing products that were easy to prepare in the stores. But were they always what customers wanted? Were we customer-centric enough?

Our customers were telling us that they wanted more than just quick and consistent. When we considered new products and tested them in limited markets, customers willingly told us whether those products were consistent with what they perceived to be the Chick-fil-A brand and whether the price point was a good value. Those fundamental questions needed to drive product decisions.

At my recommendation, Jimmy Collins agreed to move product development to the marketing department, where it remains. The goal? To keep us customer-centric.

You might ask, "Fine, but did it make a difference?" Yes, and here's an early illustration. At that time, although we were serving the best sandwich in the quick-serve category, we also offered shoestring fries that were no different from every other fast-food brand. Customer data suggested the traditional shoestring didn't match or complement the quality of the Chick-fil-A sandwich. They were a me-too product. Might our customers reward us for something better? We went to a couple of potato companies we were buying our fries from and stated we needed something innovative. Something with higher quality that was visually different, and ideally, more nutritious. Something that didn't taste like animal fat when you bit into it.

Lamb Weston had just perfected the technology to double-cut the potato to create a waffle fry, but it was not yet in the marketplace. We took that product to hundreds of customers and taste panels and got a strong positive response. Truett and Jimmy had said that we should not be serving anything but traditional shoestrings. "We're a fast-food restaurant," they said. "That's what fast-food restaurants do. It's what customers expect."

This was not a surprising response. They believed, rightly, that a menu change should not be taken lightly. We were committed to every menu item, and we would expect to be committed long term to any item we changed or added. Shoestrings were historically a nonnegotiable with a fast-food brand, and waffle fries were a more expensive, premium product with unproven added value. Perhaps even more important, customers didn't expect waffle fries from a fast-food brand; they were a paradigm buster indeed.

So we conducted in-store testing with enough stores to start seeing sales results, and we got customers' on-the-spot feedback. Would customers perceive waffle fries to be a legitimate option for french fries, while also a better-quality product, healthier, more fun to eat, and easier to eat with ketchup? They turned out to be even more popular than we anticipated, and customers saw waffle fries as a better brand fit with Chick-fil-A than shoestring french fries. In fact, many said Chick-fil-A was the only fast-food restaurant they could envision serving waffle fries. As a result, they were willing to pay more for them.

The overwhelming data made the decision easy and the brand stronger. We negotiated an exclusive deal with the company for several years before they could sell a similar product to other customers, and we introduced Chick-fil-A Waffle Fries in 1985. Truett and Jimmy were all in. Customers won the day. Fry sales boomed!

Many entrepreneurs and private family business owners would have never entertained such a major product shift. They would have stuck exclusively with the sandwich and fries that created their early success. But Truett and Jimmy listened and flexed. Today, Chick-fil-A Waffle Fries are still the number-one-sold menu item.

Customers would tell us when they wanted a change. Because

my department conducted the research that heard the voice of the customer, part of my role throughout my career at Chick-fil-A was to be their voice to leadership. When customers challenged our paradigm(s), I served as their voice. To their credit, Truett, Jimmy, and the other executive committee members were always sensitive to that voice. Their message to all of Chick-fil-A was clear: customers first.

If you keep the customer first, and you figure out how to bring the voice of the customer to the leadership table, it's not marketing's opinion any more than it is leadership's (Truett's or Jimmy's) opinion.

What do customers think about an idea? Does it make Chick-fil-A more valuable and endearing? That's what matters.

We still have food scientists, nutritionists, and chefs developing products. We have engineers and others with strong operational backgrounds all working under marketing's customer-centric banner. With every potential new product, they work in the tension between delivering what the customer wants and what the restaurant teams can prepare safely, quickly, and consistently.

We start with what is turning the customer's crank—what's getting them excited—then we try to figure out how to deliver it while making the Operators' lives as efficient and as profitable as possible.

Two More Paradigm Busters: Out of the Mall and Breakfast

The financial crisis of the early 1980s ended the wave of new mall construction, and we could not assume we would ever see another wave. We wanted to continue to offer Operators opportunities, and we wanted to control our own destiny rather than remaining subject to the whims of the financial market and mall developers. So we had to find places to build outside of malls—on the street.

Tim Tassopoulos, who was working in field operations, led a team researching our move to the street. Tim had grown up working in a Chick-fil-A store before attending Oglethorpe University and Georgetown University. We were fortunate he returned to Chick-fil-A (he now serves as chief operating officer).

Location of our first restaurants was key. We were, in effect, introducing the brand, even though Chick-fil-A had been around for nineteen years. But other than the heavy mall shoppers, nobody knew what Chick-fil-A was. Even in Atlanta, our home, the majority of people had never eaten a Chick-fil-A sandwich. Because we were introducing a brand, we could not locate in off-the-beaten-path sites. The locations would serve as major billboards for the brand and had to be easily accessible.

We ruled out locating in-line at strip shopping centers, because research showed most of our traffic, as with the malls, would be from people already planning shopping trips there. And there was virtually no visibility. We had to be visible, and we had to go right up against the big boys to find out if we could play their game, and ideally, play better than them. That led to A-grade sites, the first being at the intersection of North Druid Hills Road and Briarcliff Road in Atlanta, just off Interstate 85, in sight of a Burger King, a McDonald's, and an Arby's. (Technically, the first freestanding Chick-fil-A location was in East Point, Georgia, where Truett bought a store in 1972. But he closed that store after a few years to concentrate on malls.)

We had a prime location for our first restaurant. We would not fail because of site and a lack of traffic. Unlike every other restaurant in the chain, however, this one would be company owned and operated for the first two years, giving us opportunities to innovate and learn without putting the income of an Operator at risk.

Perry Ragsdale led design and construction to create a unique exterior look that would become an important aspect of the brand. In time, we wanted people to be able to recognize a Chick-fil-A restaurant by its silhouette.

Here's another place where Truett's brand-building insight set precedent. Years earlier, when he had developed the sandwich and selected the name, he hired a graphic designer to create a logo. The designer came back with several ideas, and Truett selected the logo we still use today, with slight variations—the name in fat script with the capital C turned into a chicken. That red logo, which was visible on a sign across the mall, really stood out in neon lights on our first freestanding restaurant.

Most of our competitors were serving breakfast in their freestanding stores, and our research with customers indicated that breakfast offered a significant opportunity for Chick-fil-A. However, Operators had kept mall hours, opening late in the morning, so they had never served breakfast. They made it clear to us that they saw more complications from breakfast than opportunities:

- Serving breakfast meant hiring additional staff to open the store earlier.
- They didn't see chicken as a strong breakfast entrée.
- They were going to be making breakfast fresh in the store every morning, increasing operational complexity.
- They feared serving breakfast would cannibalize lunch sales.

Our customer research, however, indicated that breakfast was an independent, highly loyal day part. We did our homework on competitors and learned breakfast did not cut into lunch sales. It was not uncommon for customers to eat breakfast and lunch and sometimes dinner in the same day at the same brand. "You will improve your profit margins because you'll start covering overhead earlier in the day," we explained, "and you won't be giving that day part to the competition."

Those early freestanding restaurant Operators continued to push back, so we said, "Okay. You open with breakfast and help us prove that it is either going to be a home run or a bad idea. But don't just say, 'No, we're not doing it' without at least trying it."

This is an important aspect of the Chick-fil-A franchisee relationship. Truett could have mandated that the stores serve breakfast, but that was not his preference. It wasn't our style. We would rather use personal influence than the power of position. That way we learned together, and the franchisees became highly engaged tutors for us. Also, Truett was willing for the home office to financially underwrite breakfast during the start-up period, thus giving the franchisees a "safety net" on their profit and loss statements.

In developing our breakfast menu, we believed we could again be an innovator. Our menu team, led by Dr. Baran, set out to create the first breakfast menu centered on made-from-scratch biscuits. We asked customers, "Should we offer bacon? Eggs? What if we focused on Chick-fil-A chicken for breakfast?" That seemed unusual, but then, so was the boneless breast of chicken sandwich when Truett introduced it.

Dr. Baran became "Biscuit Bill" because he spent so much time working with multiple biscuit-mix suppliers to perfect a recipe that didn't look, feel, or taste like all the other fast-food biscuits. The others reminded me of hockey pucks, because they were heavy, without a lot of flavor, often contained too much lard, and had a lot of butter on them. Bill and his team found a way to make biscuits lighter and still hold together, with a flavor profile that accented the Chick-fil-A chicken. The difference maker was one key natural ingredient that reduced the requirement for a lot of butter.

Then they put Chick-fil-A chicken inside that hot biscuit, and they had a home run. We also offered bacon, sausage, egg, and cheese options on biscuits that were kneaded, rolled, and baked in each kitchen.

One more paradigm we needed to break with our freestanding

restaurants: before 1986, Chick-fil-A was predominantly skewed to women because of the demographics of the mall shoppers. The upside opportunity as we built outside the mall was to bring the female customers with us while we attracted men and grew the base. (Today Chick-fil-A's demographic base is almost fifty-fifty.) Breakfast helped with this opportunity too.

Several weeks ahead of the first store's grand opening, Don Perry and our public relations agency, Cohn & Wolfe, were working long-range public relations opportunities, earning headlines like:

NEW FEATHER ADDED TO CHICK-FIL-A HAT

Chain Opens First Freestanding Unit Here

Then about two weeks before the opening, our marketing kicked in. We weren't spending a lot of money on media—we didn't even have billboards yet. We hit the neighborhood around the new restaurant with direct mail and door hangers. But our strongest marketing weapon, as always, was free food. We brought corporate staff to visit stores and offices in the area, giving away sandwiches, Chick-fil-A chicken biscuits, and Be Our Guest cards, communicating not only that we were opening down the street, but we were also serving breakfast. As part of that effort, we developed heated, insulated containers for transporting food and keeping it fresh and hot.

Breakfast instantly paid for itself, as did the freestanding concept for Chick-fil-A. Our first freestanding restaurant more than doubled the sales and income we had anticipated in the first year.

Throughout the years, customers have encouraged us to expand our breakfast offerings to include bagels, English muffins, breakfast burritos, fresh fruit, yogurt, and more. Most restaurants have two ovens so they can bake enough biscuits to meet demand.

With the growth of breakfast sales came requests from customers for high-quality coffee that would compete with any of the coffee shops nearby. We discovered Thrive Coffee, an Atlanta-based roaster that was buying beans direct from farmers. Their growers were predominantly small, family-owned coffee farmers throughout Latin and South America. Thrive could blend the coffee to our specifications, and when we taste tested it against Starbucks, Caribou, and even Ritz, customers rated the taste and aroma of our coffee shoulder-to-shoulder with those possessing historic cachet.

Even the coffee cup became part of the strategy, as it gave us a platform to tell the story of the independent farmers who grew the beans. We were proud to support family coffee growers who might be living in poverty if Chick-fil-A had not bought their beans.

At this writing, breakfast generates around 16 percent of sales—and restaurants stop selling breakfast items at 10:30 a.m. It's not uncommon to have restaurants that do 20 percent of their daily sales at breakfast. I think in the next five years breakfast will surpass 20 percent of sales across the chain. More people have stopped eating breakfast at home, and Operators have the capacity to grow during the breakfast day part, so they are spending more dollars and effort promoting it.

An Ownership Paradigm Buster: Grilled Chicken

Truett and Jimmy continued to build an environment within the executive committee where we were free to challenge each other—to force hard conversations, always respectfully. As a result, I am convinced the business found favor that we would not have enjoyed if we'd had an environment of avoiding conflict.

One of the hardest conversations, in fact, was whether to develop a grilled chicken sandwich.

My team and I felt that customers wanted a grilled option (because they were telling us they did), but Truett and Jimmy were concerned with disrupting the customer's relationship with the original chicken sandwich. To make his point, Jimmy called the grilled sandwich "scorched chicken," usually with a smile. My counsel to them was, "We need to hear the voice of the customer on this. Let's play this out with the customer in research, taste panels, and in-store testing. Let's see what they say and see what it does to the sales mix and the sales of the original sandwich."

The expense to ownership and the operational challenges in the restaurants would be significant—beginning with the fact that we had no grills in the restaurants. Change is not easy in a restaurant where the food is prepared in the kitchen rather than premade. Chick-fil-A restaurants were real restaurants; they made the food fresh every day. (Still do!) So when a recipe was changed or a product was added, it was not a minor issue.

Yet we were sensing that customers perceived grilled as healthier, and they wanted another option. We could talk until we were blue in the face about how many fewer calories were in the original Chick-fil-A sandwich and how low in fat it was compared to burgers and other sandwich options, but perception is reality. If some customers thought it wasn't as healthy (even though it was cooked in refined peanut oil and had half the calories of a typical hamburger), we were not going to convince them otherwise.

We needed to respond to them directly, so we developed a recipe, conducted taste panels, then took the sandwich to a few stores, then more stores, then studied the sales results. Customers let us know in large numbers that they liked the grilled option.

Grilled chicken sandwiches, the survey results showed, would add several thousand dollars to the bottom line annually for each Operator without dramatically taking sales from the original sandwich. We were reaching a new audience and also giving current customers a new reason to come more often. The voice of the customer informed our decision to go with a completely new platform of chicken entrees (the grilled sandwich, and later, salads and wraps). So, again, Truett and Jimmy listened to the customer. Chick-fil-A's first Grilled Chicken Sandwich was introduced in 1989. Results: the customers won, and the Operators won.

Commitment to Researching the Paradigm Busters

Every year, the marketing budget I submitted included funds for research. Early in my Chick-fil-A career, Truett would ask why we needed so much money for research, sometimes with a twinkle in his eye, but often he was serious.

"Truett," I said, "we're doing that for the same reason you spent five years asking people, 'How do you like the sandwich?'"

In the early 1960s when he had just one restaurant, the Dwarf House, Truett was developing the recipe for the Chick-fil-A Chicken Sandwich. He literally spent years, and with each change he sought feedback from customers.

Pickles or no pickles? Bread or bun? Butter or no butter? More or less seasoning?

"You were doing research on a much more individual, relational basis," I said. "That's qualitative research, but you were doing research nonetheless. Today, research is designed to speed up the process you took five years to do."

That research included taste panels, in-store testing, and brand performance research, and Truett was always willing to allow us to go through the process of listening to the customer in a sequential way to either validate our assumptions or not.

When you get the right customer data, and you sequentially conduct sales testing for a long enough period, you have customer feedback that provides insight into their behavior. We typically did not make any rollout decision without at least sixty to one hundred stores in a test cell, and it wasn't uncommon to in-store test a new product for a year or more. It wasn't a quick process, but that was the only way to feel good about a decision. While that was going on, we were also getting Operator feedback on procedures and processes. By the time we rolled out, we had extensive customer insights, the Operators' feedback, and impact on sales performance and Operator income.

We developed resources for restaurant leadership on how to manage inventory, how to reconfigure or reprogram the point-of-sale computer systems, and how to create marketing tools and training resources. It was all there. We could provide those resources because we went through the disciplined process of listening to customers, Operators, and the numbers.

As we expanded the chain with additional freestanding restaurants, we invested additional resources in our research to acquire customer feedback for every restaurant on product quality, service quality, cleanliness, accuracy, speed, attentiveness, courtesy—all the fundamentals of a good restaurant. We had begun those store-level benchmark studies while we were exclusively in the mall business, and then we evolved that same methodology into the freestanders.

Growth Presents Challenges We Must Address

In the late 1980s and early '90s, we opened more street stores, and customers gave us good marks on talent engagement and customer care. But on operational execution, which included consistent food quality, temperature, order accuracy, and cleanliness, they told us we were providing a wide range of performance. In other words, we weren't consistent. Some stores and Operators were absolutely nailing it, with a narrow range of disparity and a high hit rate on success. But some outliers experienced 10-, 20-, and 30-point variances of performance versus the chain mean. That was a problem. There was no use building more restaurants if we couldn't deliver consistently, because without a consistent product and experience, we were not going to be a brand. As I mentioned earlier, Truett knew long before he created the restaurant chain that the product is the fundamental underpinning of a brand. Nike better have shoes that are consistent, or it doesn't have a brand.

Chick-fil-A was no different. Dan Cathy, who was vice president of operations at the time, took responsibility. He realized this was a problem. If we wanted to grow, and if we wanted to have a viable brand, we had to deliver consistent operational excellence.

He and his team went to work and benchmarked other companies that had high levels of operational consistency, and they began to transform our standards and how we trained on those standards. They studied every detail. For example, we had standards for the way we cut lemons for fresh-squeezed lemonade or cut salad ingredients, and staff created a better process for training to those standards. To measure how well the restaurants were performing, they created in-store instruments and gave Operators the ability to hire independent mystery shoppers to give them more frequent feedback.

Over time, they completely elevated every measurement instrument in the business to execute and improve operational excellence, with the goal being zero defects. The last critical measurement, the ultimate output measurement, was our "customer benchmark data," which we were able to review by store and by market. We could go to a market and say, "Okay, you guys are performing above the mean on these measurements," or "You're outside the mean. You've still got these specific issues." Ours was a multiyear journey to reduce those operational performance gaps down to low single digits, ideally zero.

Working with research companies, we compiled similar data from our key competitors so we could compare our performance with others. We were beating many of them, but several rising stars offered formidable competition. The data helped improve our individual Operator performance and also encouraged Operators across markets to work together. Customers rewarded them with more business.

Then as we continued building more restaurants, due to customer demand we needed to put stores in areas where they started bumping up against the other existing Chick-fil-A restaurants' trading areas. We entertained for the first time a multi-unit Operator concept, where a high-performing Operator might be considered eligible for a second restaurant nearby. Customer and operational performance data, not sales and profits alone, became a crucial piece informing Operators whether they might have an opportunity for a second unit. Customers evaluating their visits told us about an Operator's ability to run a second Chick-fil-A restaurant.

Those second location opportunities helped drive operational improvement, as did the desire to be considered for a move from a mall location to a freestanding restaurant. Our attention to operational and customer measurements coincided with those new opportunities for high performers, dramatically improving and adding consistency to the brand.

Source of Sound Judgment: Wisdom

Within the executive committee, we began to realize in the early 1990s that we needed wisdom beyond our combined capabilities to manage Chick-fil-A into the future. We envisioned a time on the near horizon when sales would surpass $1 billion annually and we would have more than a thousand stores. In addition to physical growth, we had entered a time of transition around debt strategy; market penetration; brand consistency challenges; continuous differentiation, innovation, and brand relevance; talent acquisition and development; and strong Operator relationships, which included the appropriate amount of support from the home office to the restaurants. We did not want the business to outgrow our ability to manage it.

Up to that point, we had led our various areas of the company as if we were working in silos. Operations, finance, marketing, legal, and real estate were entities unto themselves. Leadership met regularly with Jimmy, and we occasionally shared information with each other. Then we returned to our departments and went back to work.

Going forward, we would become more immersed in and understanding of one another's responsibilities, and we would take on roles beyond our respective departments. This transition was a natural outgrowth of the leadership team Truett had built. We had now been working together for more than a decade—and not just working together. The men sitting around the executive committee table were among my closest personal friends. Our cohesion as a single unit rested on a foundation of caring for and trusting one another personally as we grew together professionally.

Our unity became part of Chick-fil-A's evolution from an operational company to a brand company. Early in my career, if I had tried to tell Chick-fil-A people that Chick-fil-A was a brand company, they would have thought I was nuts. But because of culture and the Operator model, we were migrating toward a healthy tension of being an operationally focused business that also wanted to use marketing to grow the business. The silos came down, and people started understanding the most important constituent was the customer, and right behind that we had the Operators serving those customers in a way that delivered the maximum brand value. We were *all* responsible for building the brand so that both of our key constituents would continue to "win."

In our prayer time before each executive committee meeting, we often spent more time praying for one another and our families than we did for the business. We were all close to the same age, and our children were growing up in similar seasons, so we prayed for children, spouses, and ourselves. We were transparent with each other about our personal concerns or needs without betraying important confidentialities.

We were similarly transparent about the business, particularly the cultural issues of the business. If someone said, "You know what, that doesn't feel right to me"—whether it was a strategic issue or a values issue—if that person could not be satisfied, we either wouldn't do it, or we'd table it. That's how much we trusted one another's judgment. My perspective was different from Buck's, whose perspective as CFO was different from Perry's in real estate and design, and so on. We learned to value each point of view.

We wanted to be more intentional about seeking God's wisdom together as we followed Truett's example. Here was a man whose formal education ended with high school, surrounded in his business by men who all had college degrees, and most who had graduate degrees. Yet he had an innate ability to make wise choices, give wise counsel, and help us determine our own wise choices.

Where did he acquire that wisdom? I'm convinced Truett's wisdom came through his study of the Bible, and he prayed for it. Perhaps without even realizing it, he lived and operated out of the wisdom made available through his faith, through what understanding he had of the Bible, and through the insight of the Holy Spirit.

His heart was already attuned to the needs of others. The Bible then guided him in ways of treating people and making decisions, what to say and what not to say, and so forth. He followed that guidance gracefully and unassumingly and without pretense. I don't remember his ever saying, "This is what God has to say about this or that." Yet more times than not, he seemed plugged in to God's perspective on issues.

In college, graduate school, and throughout my career, I read dozens of business books, and I admire the great business researchers and authors out there. I've read Jim Collins and Tom Peters, and I respect their work, along with David Aaker on brand equity and Philip Kotler on marketing. My colleagues on the executive committee were similarly committed to continual learning. But we also sought wisdom, not just knowledge.

So we explored an intentional study on the topic of wisdom, and Buck suggested we seek outside guidance. We scheduled a weeklong retreat with a professor from Wheaton College, Mark Talbot, who led us through a deep study of biblical wisdom, principally in Proverbs. Together we prayed for God's mind. We wanted His perspective. We never wanted to approach the business without the insight of the Holy Spirit. Proverbs says if you want wisdom and understanding, seek God, and then learn and glean from God's Word. So, collectively and individually, we studied and asked for it.

Through that experience, I was personally brought back to this understanding: wisdom begins with the question *why?*

I was taken back to the thought process and questions that led to the corporate purpose: Why do I exist? And why does Chick-fil-A exist? Honor God, and positive influence. By starting there, it forces me to ask *why* about any potential decision. Why do I want to do this? Will this contribute to Chick-fil-A's why, or not? Will it benefit others? Is it consistent with Truett's life verse, Proverbs 22:1 (build and protect reputation)? "Why?" forces us to pursue wisdom. We get to decide where we look for it.

SIX

Brand Journey

Preparing to Go National—with Cows

By the early 1990s, as we approached five hundred restaurants across the country, our corporate marketing efforts were still focused toward individual restaurants and markets. We began asking ourselves, "At what point do we go beyond supporting just the Operators and markets and start to position Chick-fil-A as a regional and then a national brand?"

The answer, we decided, was when we had opened restaurants in thirty-five states, and we could see that number by the mid-1990s. We were not yet to the West Coast, but we were heavily invested in Texas and had penetrated deeper into the Southwest. We were also moving into the Midwest and up the East Coast with freestanding restaurants.

As we envisioned regional and national marketing, we knew we would never be able to invest enough money in advertising to create a linear relationship between the investment and chain-wide sales.

That would have been a misguided transactional focus. We had to build the brand by creating a unique personality for Chick-fil-A that would help build top-of-mind awareness.

For nineteen years, Chick-fil-A was part of a larger destination, the mall. From a marketing perspective, opening freestanding restaurants presented an entirely new challenge. With the first street store in 1986, the issue of brand awareness and what the brand stood for leapfrogged to the forefront. While remaining sensitive to helping Operators drive sales, we would be investing in the brand with a longer-term perspective. Being part of an organization going through that marketing transition was fun and occasionally challenging for all of us, as we navigated the tension between building short-term sales and building a brand of choice.

Our mall-focused advertising agency had done a good job for us in retail merchandising, creating effective in-store graphics and menu boards. When we moved our marketing efforts outside the restaurants to billboards and radio, however, we suspected the work was not memorable enough. We sought ways to position our advertising to present Chick-fil-A as a destination brand, not just a sandwich. We knew it wasn't by showing pictures of food. Throughout the history of Chick-fil-A, a picture of the sandwich has never done it justice. It's a piece of chicken on a bun. There's no emotional connection there—nothing compelling about that.

I was a teenager in 1967 when McDonald's introduced one of its first national television campaigns with kids singing, "McDonald's is our kind of place. It's such a happy place!" Though a voice-over later in the ad would talk briefly about the food, the primary visual was happy children and their parents. Four years later Needham, Harper & Steers (an agency I interviewed with after grad school) won the account from D'Arcy MacManus with the still-famous tagline, "You deserve a break today." That line would return in 1981, my first year at

Chick-fil-A. And though "two all-beef patties . . ." pitched the best-known fast-food hamburger, the biggest chain in the world was trying to grow its brand around the experience.

When we first put our product on billboards, ours was the only chicken sandwich in the market, and that image still wasn't compelling. When others introduced chicken sandwiches, a picture of ours didn't look that much different from theirs. You could put a Chick-fil-A logo on a billboard showing the McDonald's chicken sandwich, and most people wouldn't see a difference. I'm not sure any of *you* would either. We're pretty sure McDonald's designed it that way, including the two pickles.

In addition to focusing on the food, our agency in the early 1990s was delivering lines that got lost in the crowd. Who remembers, "Wake up, your biscuits are ready"? Again, they did wonderful work in our mall restaurants, but we were concerned the creativity for brand building wasn't taking us where we wanted to go. Was it too fast-food conventional?

When we had enough freestanding restaurants in a handful of cities to move more significantly into traditional media advertising, we decided to enter into an aggressive advertising test. We engaged marketing consultant Alf Nucifora in 1993 to help us envision our advertising and creative future, then help us design an appropriate marketing infrastructure. Alf, who had served as president of two major advertising agencies, led us through a three-day marketing meeting where we created the "Market 1999 Model." We built a simulation for Atlanta that assumed one hundred freestanding restaurants and ten more in malls. Then we projected similar per-capita store penetration in Birmingham, Alabama, and Columbia, South Carolina, and created marketing and advertising strategies for those three cities based on those numbers.

To test our plan and our capacity to pull it off, we actually rolled our two-year marketing and advertising campaigns in those cities—investing as much money in marketing in 1993 as we would if we had the projected market penetration of 1999. So that the Operators wouldn't have to shoulder a dramatic increase, the company paid for all marketing expenses above 1.5 percent of 1993 sales for those three markets. A few months of experience confirmed we didn't have the level of creativity we needed to establish Chick-fil-A as a major player in the quick-serve environment.

One morning about that time, Dan Cathy boiled down the issue we were all struggling with: breakthrough creative. He asked David Salyers and advertising manager Greg Ingram, "Why don't we have better advertising? Nobody is talking about our advertising." He got no argument from us.

At this stage in Chick-fil-A's history, marketing was still not on an equal strategic footing with our operational focus. David's response cut to the chase: "If we want great creative, it's time to get a top-notch *creative* agency" (code for, "Show me the money!").

"You find the agency," Dan said. "We'll find the money."

A Different Kind of Search

Typically a company seeking an advertising agency will distribute a request for proposal (RFP) or even post an RFP on its website, inviting agencies to present portfolios and credentials. Then the company will select a group from those agencies to develop and present a pitch, which can become anything from a low-key meeting around a conference table to a parade with a marching band.

We wanted to avoid a circus atmosphere and focus instead on attributes particularly important to us at Chick-fil-A. So, instead of sending out a blanket RFP, David and Greg began to research advertising agencies across the nation who would potentially fit our culture. Like most marketing professionals, David and Greg maintained a file of creative ideas they liked and a list of agencies whose work they admired. They created a preliminary list of agencies from those files and their own experiences. List in hand, they began asking questions of other marketing leaders, like Sergio Zyman, former chief marketing officer at the Coca-Cola company. "At that point," Greg recalled, "we were making sure we hadn't left off our list any agencies we should be considering."

David and Greg narrowed their list to ten agencies from whom they sought more detailed information and samples of their work, asking them to concentrate their samples on outdoor and radio advertising. From these proposals, they narrowed their list of candidates to three agencies, including the Richards Group in Dallas, Texas.

Here is where we deviated from standard operating procedures in the advertising business. Rather than ask our top three agency candidates to create a generic pitch for Chick-fil-A, we gave them a specific assignment—to develop three-dimensional billboards (relatively new technology at the time) and a series of radio spots, so we could compare apples to apples. Our annual advertising budget was tiny, and we knew it would remain small for years to come, so the agency we selected would have to make a big impression with every creative execution. We had already determined that outdoor advertising gave us the best opportunity we could afford, and that 3-D billboards would help us create the greatest point of difference. We also believed we could make an impact with radio, given strong creative.

We invited them to work with us as if we were already doing business together. "Don't try to read our minds and figure out what we want," we said. "Ask questions; do your homework." And we paid them for their work—not a lot, but enough so they understood that we respected their thinking and we were willing to put some skin in the game. During a period of several weeks, the agencies examined the quick-service restaurant industry, talked with our customers in focus groups and one-on-one, interviewed our best Operators, observed our restaurants from both sides of the counter, and even attended our Operators seminar. We wanted them to have all the information they needed to make their best presentation.

At that point in our relationship, we were not making permanent decisions about the specific direction of our advertising. We were just trying to select an agency—evaluating the talent and their commitment. Jim Collins, in his book *Good to Great,* calls it "getting the right people on the bus." After you get the right people on the bus, then you can decide where to go.

Truett liked to say when we selected Operators, the decision is "for life." We were seeking the same kind of potential relationship with our new advertising agency. That kind of commitment is rare in the advertising world, where frequent turnover is typical, even at the highest levels of management. Most large agencies are subsidiaries of publicly held companies, so management focuses on short-term profitability, revenue streams from every client, and hours billed. It's a dog-eat-dog world where people pass continually through agencies in order to get years on their résumé so they can land a better job somewhere else. If somebody stays in a job more than three years, that's a long time. Each of those personnel changes creates a disadvantage for the client.

I also believe that clients deserve the advertising they get. David and Greg visited our three finalists and sought to evaluate their competence, their character, and the chemistry between the agencies and Chick-fil-A. They wanted to understand who was listening to us and who had their own agenda.

In the many hours they spent with the Richards Group, David and Greg saw no evidence of a short-term culture. In fact, they saw the opposite. Like Truett, Stan Richards hired people for a long-term career, and the people he hired seldom left. The Richards Group was seventeen years old at the time, and the average tenure of its creative group heads was almost nine years. Stan called his agency "The Peaceable Kingdom," after a famous nineteenth-century painting inspired by Isaiah 11 of the lion and the lamb, the bear and the ox, the leopard and the child lying down together peacefully. "We've made it our mission to tear down walls," Stan said.

David recalled, "The thing that made the difference was the chemistry we felt. All the creative work was good from all the agencies, but the Richards Group stood out in other ways. In the advertising business there can be a lot of arrogance. Not with them. We saw character in Stan Richards. Real integrity. Real devotion to the work. It didn't seem to be about the money to him—not about the dollar signs. He was all about the work! Also, it was important to us that they were privately held—an independent company like Chick-fil-A. And it was interesting to note that, like Truett, Stan Richards was a guy who would never 'retire.'"

As part of the discovery process, David wanted to learn from each of the three final candidate agencies what they expected of Chick-fil-A. We didn't have the leverage of a lot of money, so we needed the leverage of being a great client that our agency would love doing work for. "We know we'll never be your biggest client," he told each of them, "but we want to know what we need to do to be your best client."

The question struck a chord with Stan, and he paused before answering. I think he and his team cared about the question because it reflected the kind of commitment they made to their clients. We would be a great client "by respecting the work," he said. "By respecting the people who do the work and never deviating from that. That's not to say that everything we show will be a great idea. We may veer off course and miss on an idea, and you can be quick to point that out. But always be respectful. Make it a relationship between partners working hard together to get the right answer."

That exchange became an important part of "the story" of the relationship between the two companies. For more than twenty years, Stan and David told it fondly and often. After we determined the Richards Group would be our agency, David made another decision that became woven into the fabric of our story. As our team got to know the Richards Group, we became acquainted with their occasional "stairwell meetings," which were an important cultural phenomenon there. The company offices filled four floors of a high-rise in Dallas, and Stan didn't want the geography to isolate people from one another. The center of the building was designed like a four-story atrium with balconies all the way around each floor and stairways installed to connect them. Stan encouraged everyone to avoid using the elevator within the agency, and you could see the result as soon as you stepped inside, as people constantly moved up and down the staircases, stopping to talk or meet at the balcony rail. You could feel an almost pulsating energy in the motion of the place.

Stan also used the stairwell and balconies to hold impromptu meetings of the agency for special announcements or good news.

Unbeknownst to Stan, David worked behind the scenes with an assistant at the Richards Group to call a stairwell meeting. Then he showed up at the building with Chick-fil-A lunch for three hundred people and the good news of an exciting new relationship. To the entire staff in their stairwell, David made the same pledge he had made earlier to Stan: "We may not be your biggest client, but we promise to strive to be your favorite client."

That's all we could offer at the time. We felt very small compared with our competitors and our new agency's other clients. Years later Stan said, "Your promise at that point to be our favorite and best client was absolutely accurate throughout the entire relationship."

The decision to choose the Richards Group for our business was not based entirely on the creative we saw in their initial pitch. The decisive point for us was, who was going to be working on our account? Stan sat across the table from us and said he would personally see everything—every piece of creative related to Chick-fil-A. That was huge. Here was the founder and CEO of the largest privately held advertising agency in the world, committing to look at every piece of creative before his team presented it to us. He kept that promise. He also promised little turnover on the agency account management and creative team leadership (we worked with the same two creative leaders for more than a decade). It was no surprise to us in 2009 to learn that the Richards Group had been voted "Best Place to Work" in the Dallas–Fort Worth area by *Dallas Morning News*.

When David Salyers talked about the selection process, he was reminded of a lesson he learned when he joined Chick-fil-A. "I learned to ask whether my career would be about extracting value from my employer or adding value," he said. "With Stan Richards it seemed to be about the same issue. While some advertising agencies were about extracting value, he was about adding value. And when you continually add value to the business, you will stand out from the crowd and be recognized for that."

This might be a good place to note my role in this crucial selection. I served as counselor and cheerleader for David and Greg, but I intentionally stayed out of the process until they had done their work and were ready to recommend the Richards Group. I never had any second thoughts about this, because I knew David and Greg would be giving daily leadership to this important part of our brand, and they had to live with the results and the relationships, potentially for a long time. In short, I tried to empower them the way Truett empowered me, because I trusted their judgment. How good their judgment was!

From the perspective of the Richards Group, Stan saw something exciting in Chick-fil-A. He had experienced our product in our restaurants many times, and he was intrigued by the possibilities—curious about not only what Chick-fil-A was, but what Chick-fil-A could become. Stan and the Richards Group principal Brad Todd believed Chick-fil-A had built the foundational footing to be a really great brand (we agreed!), and they wanted to be a part of that. Brad had worked previously in brand management at Frito-Lay, so his roots were in building great brands. He and Stan believed—confidently—that the power of the Richards Group team and ours combined would be much greater than the two of us working separately. We were looking for much more than an advertising agency. We needed a brand-building partner that could add value to Chick-fil-A, and we found it in the Richards Group.

It's possible you saw Stan Richards's work before you ever tasted your first Chick-fil-A sandwich. Back in 1968, through a client in Dallas, Stan was hired by Twentieth Century Fox to design advertisements for an unconventional Western movie, *Butch Cassidy and the Sundance Kid*. Writer William Goldman liked Stan's ads, and when the production team in Hollywood had trouble designing the movie's opening title credits, he called Stan and asked him to give it a shot. Stan created the memorable title sequence—a flickering, sepia-toned, silent film reenactment of the Hole in the Wall Gang holding up a train, with credits appearing alongside—for the 1970 Paul Newman–Robert Redford movie, winner of four Academy Awards.

Stan never designed another movie credit sequence, but the Richards Group has produced incredibly creative work for clients like the Home Depot, Orkin, Sotheby's, Corona, Ram trucks, Fiat, and dozens more. But there is one story that does a better job of introducing the Richards Group than a long list of clients.

If I were to say the words *Motel 6*, I'm guessing the first thought in your mind would be *Tom Bodett* or maybe, *We'll leave the light on for you*. I know that because research has shown that 95 percent of Americans respond with one of those phrases when the brand is mentioned.

The Motel 6 story is one of powerful brand building with a singularly great idea, and it is one of the reasons we selected the Richards Group as our agency. Motel 6 was nearly bankrupt when the company asked the Richards Group for help. "We started with our branding process," Stan recalled, "which includes a lot of research. In this case, a lot of qualitative research."

The Richards Group went into the community and interviewed dozens of people, identified those who had stayed at Motel 6 (without tipping them off as to their client), and invited twelve of those to participate in a panel discussion.

"We were sitting behind the glass watching the interaction," Stan said, "and our account planner was at the table with these twelve people. He asked where they stayed when they were on the road, and they all said something other than Motel 6. So he went around again, asking where else they stayed, and they did it again. The third time around he began to panic, thinking he might have misrecruited the group, and finally somebody said, 'Well, if it's late at night I might stop at Motel 6, and I end up saving enough money to buy a tank of gas.' Then somebody else at the table said, 'I do the same thing and save enough to bring a gift home to my grandkids.'"

"The epiphany to us behind the glass," Stan continued, "is that they didn't admit to staying at Motel 6 because they didn't want to appear poor or cheap. But as soon as somebody else talked about it in terms of the money they saved—and we all know frugality is a good thing, while being cheap is not—others spoke up."

That idea would become the heart of the campaign. But first Stan showed his true colors by recommending that Motel 6 not advertise at all—at least not right away. "That's a hard thing for an ad agency to say," he said, "but the product was awful. To watch TV, you had to put in quarters. If you wanted to make a phone call, you had to go down the hall. We knew if we advertised and people came, they would find it woefully deficient, and they would never come back. So we waited until they upgraded the properties regionally before rolling out advertising in the same areas."

Three decades later, the key aspects of the campaign remain unchanged—a great creative idea on one dominant medium. The campaign was and is almost entirely radio based, very inexpensive compared with other media. The spots change, but the attitude remains the same. They're always entertaining, always charming, and there's always a smile in that little piece of communication. For a miniscule budget, the campaign experiences huge recall.

The Richards Group brought that same commitment to creativity for Chick-fil-A. In their proposal to earn the Chick-fil-A account, TRG wrote:

> *We believe that all our advertising should be endearing. Rewarding. Relevant.*
>
> *Our aim, when done, is to have the consumer respond:*
> *"I like what you said."*
> *"I like the way you said it." "I like you."*
> *"Let's do business."*

The foundation for the Cow campaign began to emerge in our discussions with the Richards Group during the selection process and in their research to develop their pitch. At that time, TRG's team sought to identify what they called "the most persuasive idea," a concept they utilized with each advertising execution. In the case of Chick-fil-A as a prospective client, they were looking for the single idea around which to build a campaign. The most persuasive idea:

- Capitalizes on the one advantage that no competitor can match.
- Captures the brand character and the culture of Chick-fil-A.
- Is unique to Chick-fil-A.
- Is endearing.
- Is memorable.

Through their research and interviews with Chick-fil-A customers, TRG evaluated several possible ideas: Chick-fil-A has the highest customer satisfaction of any fast-food restaurant, gives customers a tasty alternative to hamburgers, prepares everything fresh in the store daily, and tastes better because of its unique ingredients and seasonings.

Each of these ideas had an "operational excellence" bias, which was logical since Chick-fil-A had built the brand to that point relying almost entirely on operational excellence. Internally, TRG's team believed in Chick-fil-A as a healthy alternative to fast-food hamburgers. They focused on the freshness of the ingredients and the healthy nature of chicken in addition to the taste of the food. The Chick-fil-A marketing group believed our preparation method and freshness were key to distinguishing us from our competitors. And when the creative team from Richards spent time in our restaurants, they agreed. They were surprised to find that virtually everything we used was fresh, not frozen. So we started locking in on that and ran those types of ads by focus groups. The reaction we repeatedly heard from customers was, "We don't care how you make it; we just like the way it tastes." So, despite our bias that operational excellence was our strongest selling point, customers directed us away from that message.

The power of the voice of the customer proved itself time after time. Customers felt a certain ownership of the brand, and they told us what they wanted from it.

A dilemma remained, however: how to convince people who had not tasted Chick-fil-A that our products tasted great. All restaurants claimed that their products tasted better, so consumers harbored skepticism regarding that claim. That's when Brad Todd suggested a concept that became the single most persuasive idea: Chick-fil-A invented the chicken sandwich. The idea conveyed integrity, authenticity, and originality. It worked at multiple levels to establish Chick-fil-A as the chicken sandwich expert and, at the same time, subtly delivered a message of freshness and quality. Brad, with writer Doug Rucker's help, then turned the concept into a tagline that delivered the message with a smile:

Chick-fil-A
We Didn't Invent the Chicken.
Just the Chicken Sandwich.

Customers read the line and told us exactly what we hoped to hear: that if we were the inventor of the chicken sandwich, we must know a lot about it, we must be on the cutting edge, and everything else must be an imitation. And if we invented the chicken sandwich, ours must taste good. They ascribed to us the attributes we wanted under an umbrella concept of a single line, the most persuasive idea.

The Creation of "Eat Mor Chikin"

In their presentation to earn our business, the Richards team presented a dozen billboard ideas, four of them three-dimensional billboards, most of them playing off the "inventor" concept, and not a single product photo. The funniest was a giant 3-D rubber chicken on a forty-eight-foot-wide billboard with the line, "If it's not Chick-fil-A, it's a joke." We decided to make that our first 3-D execution and put it up on the main north-south artery in Dallas, Texas. Initially only the rubber chicken went up. No text or logo. Tens of thousands of people drove past, chuckled, and wondered what was going on. The volume of media chatter rose. Then we added the text and logo, and Dallas loved it so much that area Chick-fil-A Operators had T-shirts printed with the artwork and the line. They sold out. We knew we had a hit.

The next 3-D execution came in Atlanta. Two cars appeared to be driving through a billboard, and the headline promoted the double drive-thru at the adjacent restaurant. It wasn't right on message with the "inventor" idea, but with great visibility from Interstate 75, it, too, generated conversation. Operator Jason Bilotti, whose restaurant was underneath the sign, remembers seeing customers standing in the parking lot taking pictures of the board. Then, almost as if responding to Dan Cathy's earlier concern that nobody was talking about our advertising, the president of the Coca-Cola Company sent Dan a note congratulating him on the double drive-thru sign. Another city was buzzing about a single Chick-fil-A board.

What followed was a series of executions that led to the creation of the Chick-fil-A Cows. The Richards Group created a standard, two-dimensional board with a photo of a Chick-fil-A Chicken Sandwich and the line, "Don't Have a Cow!" About the same time, David Ring, the Richard Group's art director for Chick-fil-A, watched a crew on a catwalk with a ladder painting a billboard, and he began to wonder if the catwalk might somehow be used in conjunction with a three-dimensional presentation. That led to the 3-D execution of an empty ladder on the catwalk, an almost completed painting of a Chick-fil-A sandwich, and the hand-scrawled message on the board in black paint, "Boss, got hungry, back soon." A few weeks later David was on site when workers were taking down the rubber chicken from where it had debuted in Dallas.

Thinking about *Don't Have a Cow,* David realized cows wouldn't want you to "have a cow." Since Chick-fil-A doesn't serve beef, David surmised cows would be interested in what's going on there. And cows might find their own way up to that catwalk where the men had been working, and even find their paintbrush and use their ladder. (Creative types make these mental leaps!)

"You put all those things together," David recalled, "a cow, the ladder, a paintbrush, *Don't Have a Cow,* and it all leads to one thing. I don't know if anything else would have fit the bill."

David was at his desk early one morning, drawing, when all the pieces came together. He sketched a billboard with two cows on the catwalk, one sitting on the back of the other, painting *Eat Mor Chickin,* almost exactly as you've seen it a million times. "It struck me as kind of funny," David said, "but I wasn't sure what to do with it or where it fit into the campaign, which focused on the line, *We Didn't Invent the Chicken, Just the Chicken Sandwich.*" David walked over and showed the sketch to Stan, who agreed that it "seemed to contain the seed of a big idea." Stan, too, was concerned that the idea and the line did not follow the current campaign. "But sometimes," Stan said, "if it's a strong enough idea, you adapt."

TRG's creative team was not scheduled to present ideas to Chick-fil-A, but they were so excited about this one, they called and told us they were sending some ideas overnight for us to look at. They explained that one of the lines didn't precisely follow strategy, but they wanted us to see it anyway. The next morning Greg Ingram received the package and, while I was out of my office, he laid six billboard executions facedown on my desk. I returned later and turned them up one by one.

Each of the lines followed the established strategy and played off the "inventor" idea. Then I turned over the drawing of the cows painting *Eat Mor Chickin,* and I almost fell out of my chair laughing.

Greg heard me and came in, and we knew instantly that we would have to try this one. It was too good. We had no idea that morning that the Cows would become a bigger strategy idea, propelling a campaign to places we never imagined. Later we would realize it was on point, a creative innovation from the chicken sandwich innovator. A nonburger message in a burger world.

The Cow Font

Stan Richards was absolutely committed to creating masterful typography, refusing to allow this dying art to be overlooked at his agency. In his book *The Peaceable Kingdom*, Stan recalled his experience at the Pratt Institute in Brooklyn, where he learned "how to create a letter form, starting with pencil, and eventually, after an excruciatingly detailed process, finishing it with a crow quill pen. Everything had to be done by hand, and everything had to be perfect." Stan's commitment to lettering was particularly important to the Cow campaign, which relied so heavily on the "look" of the words.

"The Cow type, when you think about it, is the dominant visual," said David Ring, who created the first *Eat Mor Chickin* board. "So the same care that would go into hiring an illustrator or a photographer has to go into creating each headline. When the Cows misspell words, they try to be as phonetic as possible, but then they have to pay a lot of attention to how they space the letters. The letters within each word need to be a little closer together than usual, and the spaces between words a little wider than usual so people can read them as they drive past. Then, of course, Cows can't paint letters much better than a three-year-old, so they're not going to be consistent with their spacing."

The first billboard with the Cows spelled *chickin* with a *c* in the middle, but today, it is spelled *chikin*. So where did the *c* go?

When the Cows came inside Chick-fil-A restaurants in 1996 with their message of self-preservation, they obviously couldn't bring a forty-eight-foot-wide billboard into restaurants. They had to carry sandwich boards, which are vertical. When they painted *Eat Mor Chickin* on the vertical sign, that extra *c* forced them to squeeze the word *chickin* onto the board. They were clever enough to realize that if they dropped that middle *c*, they could make the remaining letters a little bigger and easier to read. Besides all that, Cows can't spell! The middle *c* never came back.

The Cows' Public Debut

The world was coming to Atlanta in 1996 for the Olympic Games, and we wanted them to know about Chick-fil-A. So in 1995, we signed a two-year lease on a billboard between the airport and downtown, on the right as you head into the city, and gave the Cows their world debut. For now it would be the only board we had in Atlanta with the new Cow creative. Greg Ingram remembers coming to work in a down mood one morning that week. The telephone rang, and the guy told Greg, "Hey, I'm sitting in traffic on the interstate trying to get to work, and I'm looking at the funniest billboard I've ever seen! You've totally made my day. I just wanted to tell you." Our first *Eat Mor Chikin* board had led to our first call, and it made Greg's day. And that was just the beginning. The media buzz was immediate and intense.

Then a week or so after the first board went up, Truett called and asked me to come to his office. Now, Truett almost never called me to his office, so I was thinking, *Oh, boy, this might not be good.*

When I got there, another man was in the office, and Truett introduced him to me as the executive director of the Georgia Cattlemen's Association. (What might be on his mind?) Truett was a member of the association; he raised black Angus cattle on the 260-acre farm.

We all sat down, and Truett turned to me and said, "Steve, he's concerned about our new billboard, me being a member of the Georgia Cattlemen's Association . . . what should we tell him?"

I'd known Truett long enough to know that he hadn't "given away" his position on this, and he had no intention of telling me to take it down. The ad wasn't even a campaign yet—just a single board—but it had already struck a chord.

So I said to Truett's guest, "Well, really, it's just a joke. Cows can't spell, and they're concerned about their own preservation. I can't help that. The reality is that even though Truett raises cattle, his livelihood is the chicken business. My job is to help him sell a lot of it. And those renegade cows happen to be right up our alley, so all I can tell you is, based on the way people are responding to them, it looks like they might be around for a while."

Then Truett looked at him with a little smirk that he might have been trying to politely hide and said, "Well, yeah, I think Steve's probably right."

We both knew we were onto something big.

Expanding the Cows' Reach

We were so excited about the Cows and *Eat Mor Chikin* that we wanted to get them up in more markets immediately. I went to Jimmy Collins and said, "We've finally broken through with something that's going to have legs, if you'll pardon the pun. But we need to get it up in more markets to get a true sense of its potential."

At the time, our top twenty markets represented two-thirds of sales throughout the chain, and all of them had at least one freestanding restaurant. Jimmy understood our strategy was about building the brand by creating word of mouth, not telling folks where to turn. To get that many boards up, the company would have to subsidize the markets four hundred thousand dollars above their 1.5 percent (of sales) media contribution. That would give us enough to pay for fabrication of the Cows and keep them up for ninety days. If the markets' Operators liked the results, they would be asked to keep the Cows' messages up for at least two years if we made this investment. Jimmy didn't hesitate. He gave his full support.

Soon after we installed a 3-D board in Chattanooga, some teenagers stole the set of Cows. Local media turned it into a funny news story, then CNN picked it up and went international with it. Don Perry, Chick-fil-A vice president for public relations, put out a press release saying we would not press charges if the Cows were returned safely. They were, and we wound up getting more media coverage than we ever could have imagined. Many years later, I was playing golf with a friend in Florida, and one of his buddies confessed to knowing one of the two teenagers who "stole" the Cows. I gave him a high five, a free Chick-fil-A sandwich card, and a huge *thank you*. "He helped launch our campaign!" I said.

Later we conducted our annual research to find out what people had seen and what they remembered from Chick-fil-A advertising. At the time, we had about thirty billboards around Atlanta, all of them showing food, and we had the one *Eat Mor Chikin* billboard. The research showed the single Cow billboard was more memorable than all the other boards combined. It had 80 percent recall! People remembered the characters that made them laugh, and because of the iconic nature of the Cows, they remembered Chick-fil-A.

The *Eat Mor Chikin* board, even though we had one board up in each of twenty markets, was still a single outdoor execution, just like the rubber chicken and the double drive-thru. We began to wonder if the *Eat Mor Chikin* moment might have the potential for becoming a *movement*. David Salyers, Greg Ingram, and I met with Stan Richards and Brad Todd and talked about the possibility of the Cows becoming a campaign. "What a great way to take friendly potshots at the burger guys," we said, "almost without people knowing we're doing it." Using the Cows would also allow us to get away from the food industry's preoccupation with food photography. Stan asked us to give his group three months to develop ideas for a campaign built around the Cows.

Not everybody found the Cows funny. Over the years, both Truett and I would receive letters from teachers complaining about the Cows misspelling words, and I responded with a standard letter: "We're sorry, but Cows can't spell. It's just a joke. Maybe you could use it as an object lesson to help kids learn the right way to spell. Thanks for what you do!"

The Power and Responsibility of an Icon

How many times have you experienced this: you're watching television and see a commercial you really like, but someone asks you two minutes later who the advertisement was for, and you can't remember?

With an icon, that doesn't happen. As soon as you see a duck, a gecko, a pink toy bunny—or a Cow—you know the sponsor. We never told, or even expected, the Richards Group to create an icon for Chick-fil-A, but when we discovered they had, we latched onto it.

We approached the Cows' celebrity status with the perspective of a talent agent. A celebrity has to be in the limelight all the time to remain relevant. An actor from twenty years ago isn't as interesting as one from a movie you saw last week. For this campaign to work, we had to use the Cows everywhere, not just on a billboard and an occasional television spot. The Cows had to become so fully integrated in their campaign of self-preservation that it was not surprising to see them fall out of the rafters at the Chick-fil-A Bowl. It was not surprising that a Cow would stick his sign in your face on a CBS or ESPN broadcast. If they didn't show up everywhere, from the top of the marketing pyramid to the bottom, they would not be an icon. They had to be relentless.

Many valuable, iconic campaigns have been abandoned, to the detriment of their owners. Tony the Tiger and the Pillsbury Dough

Boy were both cast aside only to be resurrected years later. Even the Green Giant, named by *Ad Age* the third-most recognizable ad icon of the twentieth century,[7] left television for years. He was brought back in late 2016 with a backstory explaining that he had been away creating new, healthier products. That's the power of an icon.

The marketing department and Chick-fil-A Operators worked like Hollywood agents to keep the Cows out front, "booking" them for appearances at local events or on media. Why else would a child, teenager or adult want their photo taken with a Cow? Cows have to be cool. They need their icon status to create opportunities to propagate their message and their humor. We invested in the Cows to make them a personality, then we leveraged their celebrity status to take us from where we were to where we wanted to be. A lot of marketing departments at a lot of companies around the country would love to have an icon with the personality and star power of the Chick-fil-A Cows. We were blessed and we knew it.

We also stayed in our lane with regard to the creative aspect of the campaign. In twenty years working with the Richards Group, neither I nor anyone else in the Chick-fil-A marketing department suggested a punch line for an ad. That was the Richards Group creative team's job, and they were much better at it than we were. Plus, we didn't want to create a strategic struggle on whose idea was better. If we thought an idea they presented didn't work or could be improved, we asked them to try again.

Three Great Advertising Lessons

In my opinion, three virtues apply to any advertising that is truly brand building.

The first is *engaging*. It can't be missed. It grabs your attention.

Immediately, one knows that's X, Y, or Z's brand. I know that's Chick-fil-A. Or, I know that it's Aflac. That's engaging!

Then it's *endearing*. People grow to love the advertising to the degree that they look forward to seeing the next execution. Endearing makes the brand a unique part of their life emotionally, even when they're not engaged physically with the brand. That was one of the virtues of the Cow campaign. Endearing!

And it's *enduring*. It has the creative underpinnings for a long run with multiple creative executions of the campaign. And because it's a campaign, it represents good stewardship. There's Cow creative one could pull off the shelf right now that was created years ago, and it would still work. It isn't dated. It really stretches the financial investment. That's enduring!

Real Cows

We faced the challenge of bringing the Cows into the restaurants, and our first inclination was to create cartoon cows. We even contacted Gary Larson, creator of *The Far Side* comic and the cows that inhabit his world. Fortunately, he declined the opportunity, because in hindsight, it wouldn't have worked. Nobody eats cartoon hamburgers. If the hamburgers are real, the Cows should be real in order to convey the jeopardy.

A member of The Richards Group team suggested contacting a photographer he knew who took photographs of animals, usually dogs, and altered them digitally to put them in human-like situations. "Why not shoot actual cows," the Richards Group reasoned, "and get them to do things?" The first thing they showed us was a replica of a seven-foot-tall Cow wearing an "Eat Mor Chikin" sandwich board. We knew immediately that was the answer. We debuted these "standing" Cows (with their painted signboards) in restaurants in July 1996 on multiple point-of-purchase materials, and within a couple of weeks customers had taken so many of them, we had to print more. We were thrilled! No one had ever taken our photographs of sandwiches or salads home with them. Now they were taking Chick-fil-A advertising and putting it in their homes and offices.

Years later the Cows are still finding ways to surprise the public. After seeing Chick-fil-A Cows hanging from water towers or climbing the "fowl" poles at Minute Maid Park, where the Houston Astros play baseball (and won the 2017 World Series), people sometimes ask, "How did they get away with that?" Getting away with it started by having a great creative team at the advertising agency who thought like children, and having media partners who were willing to be creatively flexible on potential execution applications.

Dominating the Category

A key factor in the success of Chick-fil-A throughout the chain's history has been the ability to dominate particular categories, even with an extremely limited budget. The obvious example is the first: Truett created the boneless breast of chicken sandwich and for more than a decade it remained uncontested.

By pioneering fast food in shopping malls, Truett once again established Chick-fil-A as the dominant player in this environment where the chain would flourish.

Moving outside the malls meant going head-to-head with companies that spent more in a week promoting their brands than Chick-fil-A spent in a year. What marketing category could we dominate that they had not already claimed?

Most fast-food advertising is TV driven. Other media are

secondary. With our limited budget we couldn't go head-to-head with them on TV. We decided instead to try to dominate outdoor advertising as a brand builder. Even in that category, we knew that the major players would spend millions more than we ever would.

Fast-food billboards traditionally pushed a price point or told potential customers where to turn. The industry used other media to build their brands while utilizing billboards to influence the location of transactions. We went against the prevailing thinking by using billboards to build our brand. As the only fast-food chain utilizing the medium for brand building, we believed we could dominate with smart execution.

Chick-fil-A's domination of billboards for brand building never had, and never could, rely on plastering more boards in a market than our competitors. In Atlanta in 2009, for example, we had fewer than twenty 3-D boards for a metropolitan area of more than five million people. We won by putting a limited number of boards in high-traffic areas, with creative that people talked about. High visibility, high impact, always remembering it's the *quality* of the impression, not the *quantity*.

These billboards were working 365 days a year. In a major market we could buy a spectacular board location alongside an interstate highway for a year, or we could buy six or seven weeks of television advertising. The agency's job, then, was to develop creative that worked all day, every day.

How did we evaluate creative? It wasn't complicated. Every execution had to make us laugh. It had to be endearing. At the same time, every use of the Cows had to be appropriate. There had to be an element of self-preservation on the Cows' part, and the jokes had to align with Chick-fil-A's culture. We couldn't show anything mean-spirited or that got too close to barnyard humor.

We thought of the Cows as seven-year-olds. That was their mentality. Because of that, there's not a lot we came up with that would be inappropriate for Chick-fil-A as a company. But sometimes one of our creative groups would cross a line into an area that wasn't right for the brand. Or they would create something that was too sophisticated for the Cows. We wanted to make sure the joke wasn't one that only a twenty-five-year-old would get. The humor had to be broader than that—charming, endearing, and funny to a sixty-year-old as well as a six-year-old.

Never a Shill for the Brand

We also took great care ensuring the Cows never became shills for Chick-fil-A. They were in this thing for their own self-interest, not Chick-fil-A's. If their work started to look too much like they were advertising *for* Chick-fil-A, such as promoting specific products and ingredients, they would quickly lose their edginess and even their believability.

One of the biggest challenges came when we introduced new products, and we were tempted to ask more of the Cows. We had to be careful not to expect the Cows to do too much. It made perfect sense for them to say, "Eat Mor Chikin," but we didn't expect them to say, "Drink more milkshakes."

As I shared earlier, shortly before Jimmy Collins retired as Chick-fil-A president, he said at our Operator seminar, "It's easier to become a success than to remain one. Be careful." He was speaking of the chain, but the statement was true for the Cow campaign. It was easier to create it than to maintain it. Our goal was for people to feel, either consciously or subconsciously, *I like those folks at Chick-fil-A. I don't know where they come up with that advertising material, but that is funny stuff.* Then when they were hungry, Chick-fil-A was one of the first places they remembered when they were deciding where to eat.

With all this in mind, the Richards Group wisely created the *Chick-fil-A Moo Manifesto* to serve as guardrails for the campaign. I suspect any client and agency managing an iconic campaign has something similar.

The Chick-fil-A Moo Manifesto

As the Chick-fil-A Cow Campaign evolves, we should ensure that all creative executions hold fast to these few but crucial (like the two pickles on the Chick-fil-A Chicken Sandwich) criteria.

The Cows Always Act in a Renegade Manner

These aren't your garden-variety Holsteins. These guys pop up in places where you least expect them: on a billboard, taking over the airwaves, or even on the city's water tower. They know that if they don't continue to surprise and entertain us, they become boring and expected, which is one step away from becoming *burgers*.

The Cows Are Not on the Chick-fil-A Payroll

They are more believable, more endearing, and just plain funnier if they always act purely in the interest of self-preservation. They happen to endorse Chick-fil-A simply because Chick-fil-A makes the best chicken, thereby increasing the odds that people will choose poultry over beef. Uncomfortable as corporate pitchcows, they do their best to stay away from any company emblem. The only logo they would ever consider wearing is ours because it helps their cause. Fact is, they'd be offended if any company gave them money. Besides, they have no pockets.

The Cows Have a Fairly Simple Sense of Humor

They don't believe in elaborate productions. Theirs is a "grassroots" effort, so they always opt for the simplest, most economical way to get their point across. They'll just mow (or eat, if necessary) the grass in their field, or they'll grab a bucket of paint and a brush. And their humor is marked by naïve silliness. Some would say stupidity. But that's not very nice.

The Cows, with Increasing Frequency, Are Awkwardly Anthropomorphic

While originally content to stand on their own four feet, lately the Cows have dressed up their message in more and more human terms. Which translates into a steady reliance on costumes and awkward impersonation. None too subtle (to us, anyway), their clumsy attempts to infiltrate human culture are nonetheless admirable. Ridiculous, but admirable.

The Cows Can't Spell

Oh, they give it their best shot. But cows aren't the smartest creatures in the world, especially when using someone else's language. Their grammar isn't so hot, either. And they smell funny.

The Cows Are Low-Tech

When they manage to use technology, they use it in the most rudimentary and sometimes wrong way. They're low-tech because they have hooves instead of fingers, they weigh about five hundred pounds, and they rarely read the instructions.

The Cows Are Not Always Politically Correct

Years ago, the Cows figured out that people want to eat them. Suffice it to say, they're a little miffed. As such, they'll stop at nothing to get their message across. Remember, they don't work for Chick-fil-A, so they might "say" and do things we wouldn't. While savvy enough to understand that offending us humans can backfire, they're certainly willing to cross the line from polite to pointedly frank. ("Lose That Burger Belly" comes to mind.)

If we keep these simple guidelines in mind when creating and judging our ads, the ads will be better, the chicken will sell faster, and the Cows will be much, much happier.

And over the long haul, because of this strategic clarity, we had an iconic campaign, not just a bunch of ads. A campaign that was engaging, endearing, and enduring! What a gift, and what fun!

Awards and Honors for the Cow Campaign

The Cow campaign was not only rewarding in terms of sales and engagement, but it received many awards and honors over the years, such as the OBIE, two EFFIEs, being added to two halls of fame and the Smithsonian American History Museum. Stan Richards was inducted into the American Advertising Hall of Fame in 2017, and the Chick-fil-A Cow campaign was noted as one of his career milestones.

SEVEN

Connecting with College Football Fans

Concurrent with the beginning of our search for a new advertising agency, we recognized a new opportunity to build a national brand beyond the South and Southwest, an opportunity that fit Chick-fil-A's and Truett's personalities perfectly. This opportunity would lead us all the way to the College Football Playoff. And it began with women's professional golf. Yes, golf.

Truett's friend J. T. Williams wanted to bring an LPGA event to his Eagle's Landing golf community south of Atlanta, and he needed sponsors. Truett wanted Chick-fil-A to help. I wasn't sure the brand was big enough to take on an event of that magnitude, but we looked into the possibilities and decided to try to make it work for the LPGA, Chick-fil-A, and Atlanta's Southside.

The first LPGA tournament that Chick-fil-A sponsored in 1992 was our opportunity to "activate" our food and people and to engage our vendor partners. Extending our hospitality beyond the restaurants to the golf course introduced the brand to many of the patrons for the first time. The event was in the heart of Chick-fil-A territory, just twenty miles from our home office, but it attracted visitors, pro-am participants, media, and LPGA players from around the United States and the world. Many of them had never heard of Chick-fil-A. In the process, we were learning how to produce and leverage sponsored events. It was also scheduled to be part of ESPN's coverage of the LPGA.

Within a few years, the Chick-fil-A Charity Championship hosted by Nancy Lopez became one of the most popular and charitable stops on the LPGA Tour, in no small part due to Nancy's support and personal involvement. Our success with this event encouraged us to investigate other potential sports partnerships. With more than five hundred restaurants in more than twenty markets, we could consider an event that would give us some bigger national exposure, or at least significant regional visibility. We looked at NASCAR, the PGA, Major League Baseball, and the NFL, and in every one of those possibilities we saw audience waste or inefficiency and the requirement for activating on Sundays—a nonstarter with all our stores closed on Sundays.

We studied independent research and learned that Chick-fil-A customers were 40 percent more likely to watch a college football game on TV than were customers of other fast-food restaurants. We also learned that people actually attending college football games were *six times* more likely to eat at Chick-fil-A than at other fast-food restaurants. An amazing demographics fit. We felt we had to find a way to take advantage of this clear and powerful connection. Efficient, passionate fans, no Sunday issues, appointment TV.

On December 31, 1993, Dianne and I had a New Year's Eve date to the Peach Bowl, Clemson versus Kentucky. (If you love college football, it can be a date!) Sitting in the upper deck looking around the Georgia Dome, I saw several thousand empty seats. But the atmosphere was great. The game had come a long way from its founding by the Lion's Club of Atlanta in 1968 to its near extinction in the mid-1980s. The game had been played outdoors, first at Georgia Tech's Grant Field and then at Atlanta–Fulton County Stadium, often in bad weather. In 1985, fewer than thirty thousand fans sat in a cold, driving rainstorm to watch Army beat Illinois. CBS pulled its contract, and the game itself was at risk because it barely met the NCAA minimum requirement for local ticket sales. The Atlanta Chamber of Commerce then took over management of the game and convinced major corporations of its importance to the community. Delta, Coca-Cola, Home Depot, and Georgia Power all became sponsors. The Georgia Dome opened in 1992, and the game moved indoors. A year later, Dianne and I watched from the upper deck.

"I'm amazed this game doesn't have a title sponsor," I said. "If nothing else, the right title sponsor could help them fill this building."

"Well, why don't you do it?" she said, meaning Chick-fil-A, of course.

She'd known what I was thinking. Why not Chick-fil-A? The Peach Bowl had virtually zero audience waste for us, not only in terms of demographics and geography, but also on-site brand activation; and it had tentacles that could move us into college towns, college alumni associations, athletic departments—unbelievable relationships that Operators could partner with in their communities. The timing was almost perfect, as we had just started licensing Chick-fil-A restaurants on college campuses, and an affiliation with college football might add energy and momentum to those opportunities.

The majority of our restaurants were geographically in the crosshairs of the Atlantic Coast Conference and the Southeastern Conference, great college football territory, and coincidentally, the Peach Bowl had penned a long-term agreement with the ACC and the SEC to host two of their teams in the Georgia Dome every year.

"Of course," I said. "You're right, babe." And for the rest of the game I sat back and considered the possibilities.

The following week, I met with David Salyers and other members of our team and shared my thoughts. We weren't thinking national at that time. Seventy percent of our stores were in the footprint of the SEC and ACC, so we were thinking about the teams coming to this ballgame as well as the students, fans, and alumni watching on ESPN.

Even before presenting the idea to Truett, we were following his lead. Truett had an innate, intuitive sense for what he wanted the Chick-fil-A brand to be. Implicit in that, he could discern what fit and what didn't fit. I had studied him carefully, and after fifteen years in the business, I had become a big fan of using data to inform decisions but knew not to let it make the decisions for us, particularly when dealing with a brand attempting to genuinely connect with our customers. "Informed intuition," as I liked to call it, provided a sense of what might add brand value for Chick-fil-A, based on both facts and emotional "fit." College football hit the bull's-eye for both.

And then there was energy. Energy attracted Truett, especially the energy of young people. He was fine around the adults in the restaurants, but he gravitated first toward children, always asking, "What do the Cows say?" Then he turned to the teenagers working behind the counters. When he was well into his eighties, he still connected with their energy. He wanted passion and energy in and around Chick-fil-A, and since college football is the epitome of energy, the connection between Chick-fil-A and college sports was a natural extension of Truett's personality. And an added bonus: I love the game too!

We decided to pursue the possibility of becoming the title sponsor of the game. Robert Dale Morgan, who was the Peach Bowl's executive director, and two board members (Albert Tarica and Bob Coggins) listened to our sponsorship idea, but their response was lukewarm at first. They were particularly concerned by the possibility of title sponsor turnover, changing the name of the game after two or three years, which was common in the bowl business at that time.

They were not yet familiar, however, with one of the most important tenets of Chick-fil-A's culture: commitment. Truett Cathy and Chick-fil-A didn't make short-term decisions with Operators, employees, suppliers, or corporate partners. After we did our homework and made a commitment, we were all-in with every relationship. The net result: create a long-term, win-win situation for both parties.

"What if we guarantee you a minimum three-year deal with an option to renew for another three years?" I asked. "If you don't like it, you don't have to renew it. We don't like it, we don't have to renew. In other words, how about a potential six-year deal?" Now they were listening.

That meeting was the first of many over several months as the bowl's leadership grew more comfortable with the idea and we negotiated a fee schedule and related rights.

We agreed to a lower fee the first year that would grow over time, mirroring Chick-fil-A's anticipated growth. We also committed to buy the ten commercial spots on ESPN that the bowl was contracted to sell. Our first national television.

"We'll help you sell out the game and promote viewership," I said. We didn't want to put the Chick-fil-A name on anything that was not a total success. We saw the bowl as a potential Chick-fil-A brand asset. Robert Dale became convinced and advocated for the deal and co-branded marketing effort.

After negotiating most of the key components of a deal with the Peach Bowl, I was ready to lay out the opportunity before the nine-member Chick-fil-A executive committee. This was an expensive, long-term commitment, and as a business, we hadn't fully made the philosophical transition from selling chicken to building the Chick-fil-A brand. There was strong sentiment that we might be too early.

But my philosophy was that you don't start promoting a regional brand when you *are* a regional brand. Rather, you start promoting a regional brand *before* you want to be a regional brand. Likewise, you start promoting yourself as a national brand *before* you're a national brand.

At the meeting where the executive committee had to make a decision, I explained the deal and said, "We need to understand that I believe we don't do this deal unless we're in it for the long haul. Because we're not going to build brand affiliation—we're not going to make the bowl and Chick-fil-A a new 'brand'—unless we make a long-term commitment. If we aren't willing to go on this ride and assume it's at least six years, and see how it performs for the business, then don't support it. Our investment cost will grow year by year, and hopefully the size of the business will grow proportionately so it won't financially constrain us. But, obviously, I can't guarantee that."

"This is a brand investment," I said, "doing for the Operators what they cannot do for themselves. Only the home office can do this."

They were not all convinced. But we were at a point where we had to give the bowl our decision. So the executive committee voted—four in favor and four opposed. Truett had listened but not voted.

Then Jimmy Collins, who had supported the deal, turned to him and said, "Well, Truett, what do you think?"

"Sounds like a good idea to me," he said. "I think we ought to do it."

On December 31, 1996, Truett stood at midfield with the captains from LSU and Clemson to announce that the Chick-fil-A and Peach Bowl partnership would start the next season. Our journey to becoming a national brand had just taken an important step. At the same time, the Richards Group was expanding the Cow campaign. The Chick-fil-A brand would never be the same.

To get ready for the first Chick-fil-A Peach Bowl, we brought in George Hirthler's agency to help us brand the new partnership. I had admired his work for the 1996 Centennial Olympic Games in Atlanta, so when it was time to create a brand look for the bowl, George and his team were a perfect choice.

After our first Chick-fil-A Peach Bowl, the 2000 Atlanta Super Bowl host committee recruited and hired Robert Dale to become its executive director. The Peach Bowl committee, in turn, hired Gary Stokan, who played basketball and was later an assistant coach at North Carolina State. Gary had worked in corporate sports management at Adidas and Converse and had owned and operated two sports marketing companies. He and his new team, and our team, began meeting together at least monthly. A joint brand journey had begun.

Then we expanded our exposure with college athletics by becoming a corporate sponsor with the SEC and the ACC. That gave us access to all their events and the respective fans who attended. Engaging personally with fans at the SEC Championships and ACC Championships in football and basketball became a great opportunity for us to make connections on the ground, face-to-face. But after a few years, the conferences told us we couldn't activate directly with fans through our food and people the way we had been.

So we pulled out of some of the conferences' events and used that money to supplement a new deal with CBS's SEC college football schedule. About the same time, we were reviewing the impact of the Chick-fil-A Charity Championship with Nancy Lopez, the LPGA event we had sponsored since 1992. The event, we believed, could take off if we could make some changes, including moving it to the East Lake Golf Club, which became the permanent home of the PGA Tour Championship in 2004. When we were unable to make traction with our desired changes, we realized that we needed to move away from the LPGA event after an eleven-year run. Again, we used that money to supplement the advertising commitment on CBS and ESPN. We were able to start buying portions of the whole college football season with both networks. Our awareness numbers responded strongly, and Operators said they felt this new visibility was positively impacting their sales. Same-store sales were growing.

We wanted to be more than just a pay-for-play advertiser, and the creative team at the Richards Group was always looking for new ways to leverage the Cows. One of those possibilities was to convince ESPN and CBS to let us show creative that could run during the game broadcast, not just another thirty-second ad. The Richards Group created and proposed what I call "in-game ditties," those fun things the Cows like to do, such as present the starting lineups and impact players. They were created in the same spirit and strategy as the ads themselves, and we had to meet the network's standards for how long they could be on screen and graphically where they came in or went out. But in terms of the flavor and tone, they were an extension of the Cows' renegade campaign. They were making people smile during the game broadcast.

Why not? This was part of the fun and the nuance of building a brand around emotional value and not just transactional value. We weren't running commercials to promote any given product or a special price for the next thirty days. We were doing something to make you like Chick-fil-A. Stan Richards often said, "The most enduring brands are the brands that are endearing."

We had to negotiate prices for those "ditties," but when CBS's Verne Lundquist, the Hall of Fame broadcaster, laughed while announcing, "Bring on the Cows," we knew we'd found another winner. If we could make Verne laugh, that might be better than saying something nice about us. Besides, he had a contagious laugh.

Building Friendships

The Chick-fil-A Peach Bowl not only built our brand's support base but also led to new relationships with athletic directors and coaches that were crucial to our growth in the college football space. Dianne and I built friendships professionally and personally that have stood the test of time.

In 2001, Auburn played North Carolina, and Dianne and I hosted Auburn's athletic director, David Housel, and his wife, Susan, and head coach Tommy Tuberville and his wife, Susan, at our home for dinner as a respite from the crowds. During the evening, Tommy shared with us the positive influence that his full-time team chaplain, Rev. Chette Williams, had on his players. Historically, the Fellowship of Christian Athletes (FCA) provided chaplains to work with athletes on high school and college campuses, but Tommy had someone dedicated solely to his Auburn football players. Chette, a former Auburn player, was a father figure, friend, mentor, pastor, and role model for young men who, in many cases, had grown up without a father in their home. Coaches simply didn't have time to fill all those roles, Tommy explained, and the nature of the coach–player relationship required a certain distance because of the discipline involved.

David explained that because FCA raised money from donors to pay for Chette's salary, office rent, and expenses, there was no conflict with the Auburn administration. This conversation raised Dianne's and my interest and spurred our first involvement with and support of FCA, continuing today, even in our family—our son-in-law joined the FCA Atlanta staff in 2015.

Soon after that first dinner, Gary asked if Dianne and I would host another dinner the next year, this time with the head coaches and athletic directors from both schools. We readily agreed, and in 2002, Phillip and Vicky Fulmer, from Tennessee, and Ralph and

Gloria Friedgen, from Maryland, joined us for a dinner that became an annual tradition of hosting the opposing coaches, athletic directors, and their wives before the game—away from the competition, distractions, and pressure of the bowl week.

Licensing Chick-fil-A on College Campuses

The Chick-fil-A Peach Bowl also supported our expansion of Chick-fil-A's licensed restaurants onto college campuses. "Licensed" meant we had to work with concession contractors who held the food-service rights on a campus. Those deals came together more easily as we gained greater visibility within college athletics. At this writing, Chick-fil-A has licensed restaurants on more than 250 college and university campuses.

College locations represented an opportunity to develop a future customer franchise for the brand by potentially exposing Chick-fil-A to people who otherwise had never experienced it.

Initially, because of problems he'd had with his early licensing experience with the Chick-fil-A sandwich, Truett had reservations with the concept, which turns over the production of our product to another company. But our team, led by Jack Sentell and Barry White, designed a model where a local Chick-fil-A Operator was directly involved in training and verifying the quality of the licensed operation. Those locations became principally about building the Chick-fil-A brand and creating trial, while also creating another income stream for the partnered Operator from the license fee. Later the program expanded even further, to include licensed partners in hospitals and airports.

Abducted Cow Alive And Well But Still Lost

By LANCE COLEMAN
Free Press Staff Writer

Where's the beef?

That's what people in the Chattanooga are asking following the early Sunday morning heist of one of the plastic 5-by-8-foot Holstein cow statuettes perched on the Chick-Fil-A billboard on Highway 153.

And several people evidently know where the cow is.

During interviews with shoppers at Hamilton Place Mall on Tuesday night to get their reaction to the theft, one shopper revealed that he knew where the cow was. But he wanted to remain anonymous and not be involved.

He said he wasn't involved in the theft, but overheard some friends talking about the incident.

The shopper was given a camera and asked if he would go to where the cow was and take a picture.

He obliged.

He returned the camera and the film to the *Free Press* late Tuesday night. The picture shows three "rustlers" hiding their identity while posing with the cow.

"We've had several phone calls of people calling in saying 'We know where your cow is,' or just saying 'Moo'," said Dean Kirstein, owner and operator of the Chick-Fil-A at Northgate Mall. He said the

See COW, Page A2

BOVINE BANDITS: This photograph was delivered anonymously to the *Free Press* Tuesday night and appears to show the large plastic Holstein cow taken from a Highway 153 Chick-Fil-A billboard. Chick-Fil-A officials have said they will not press charges against whoever took the cow if it is returned.

A newspaper in Chattanooga, Tennessee, reported a story about two of the five-by-eight-foot plastic cows stolen from a Chick-fil-A billboard. It was picked up by CNN and went international.

First licensed location. Georgia Tech campus, 1992.

First Chick-fil-A Peach Bowl logo, 1997.

The beginnings of Chick-fil-A: The Dwarf Grill, established in 1946.

The Dwarf House now sits where the original Dwarf Grill once stood.

First mall restaurant. Greenbriar Mall, Atlanta, Georgia, 1967.

First free-standing restaurant. North Druid Hills Rd., Atlanta, Georgia, 1986.

The Cows campaign started with a sketch. This one is by art director David Ring © The Richards Group.

Photo of original art rendering of the first Eat More Chickin board. Started with two c's in *chikin*.

First trial of a 3-D billboard, Dallas Turnpike, 1995.

The forty-foot Cow at Turner Field, Atlanta, Georgia, one of many Cow sightings at Major League Baseball parks.

First use of nontraditional outdoor billboards, I-85S entering Atlanta.

First restaurant in Manhattan, New York, 2015.

Cow campaign recognized on the Madison Avenue Advertising Walk of Fame in New York City.

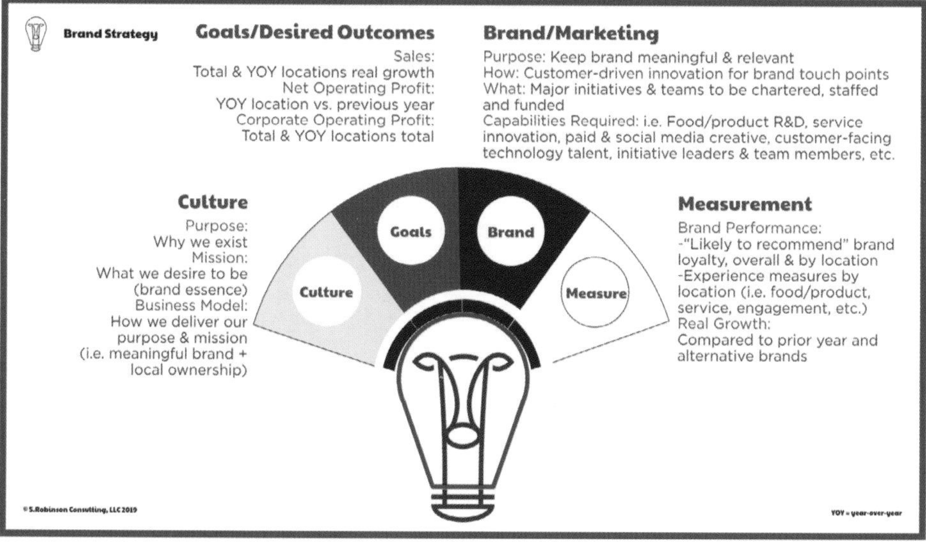

This is a high-level "box top" of the key components of the brand and marketing plan. Built left to right.

Srobinson Consulting LLC

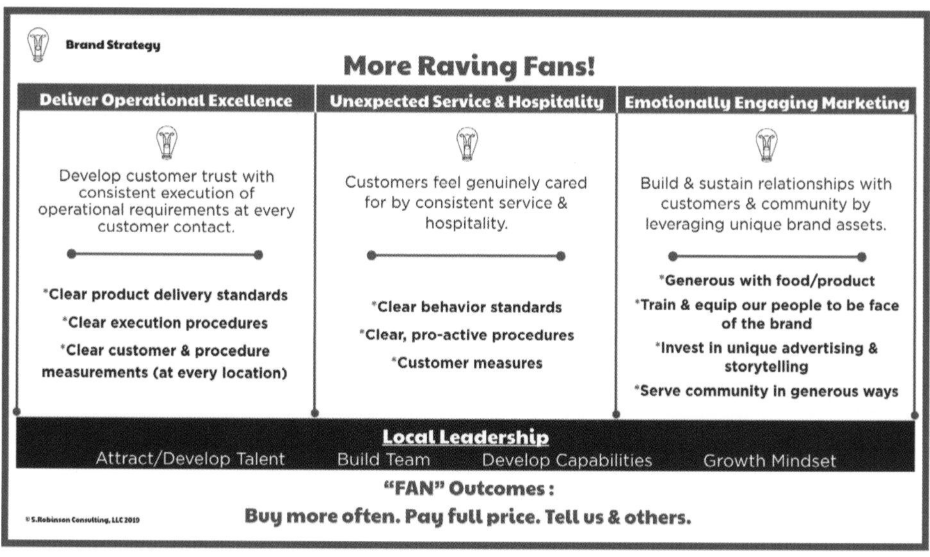

This visual captures the critical components of a customer relationship–building strategy, similar to that developed at Chick-fil-A. The role of the marketing department at the home office was to develop ongoing innovation, plans, and infrastructure that would assist Operators. Clearly, Chick-fil-A Operators are the foundation of Chick-fil-A's ability to activate this strategy.

Srobinson Consulting LLC

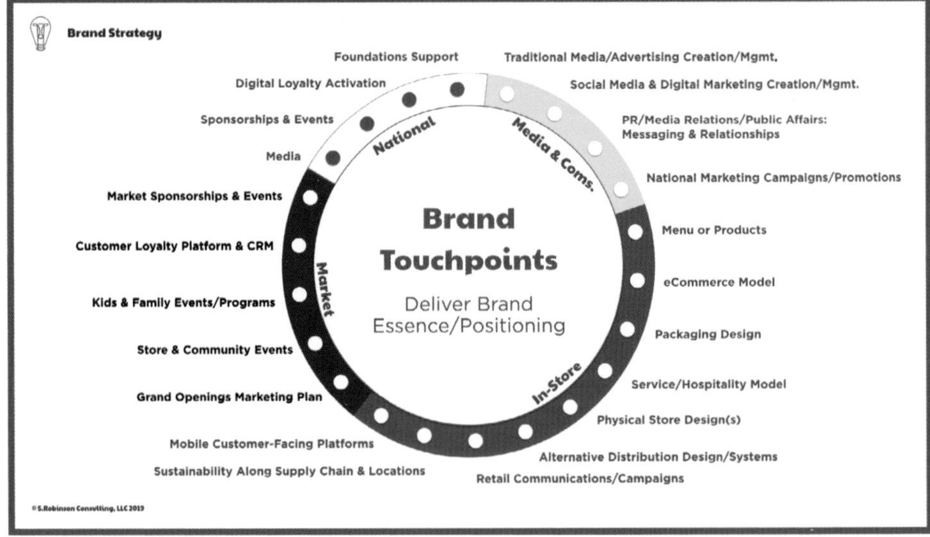

For more than thirty-five years, the marketing department grew in its support of the business, evolving beyond traditional marketing disciplines to total brand development. This visual is a snapshot of how we made that happen. Every dot on this circle represents a potential initiative in an overall business plan, each one dependent upon a department or business-wide, cross-functional team accountable for that piece of the plan and its execution. Each team had a C-level sponsor and team facilitator.

Srobinson Consulting LLC

A postcard Steve sent to the Chick-fil-A marketing team from the Rose Bowl. A Chick-fil-A billboard is behind him in the end zone. It felt like a national brand launch that day, January 1, 2015.

Brenda Green and Don Perry offering PR counsel to Truett and Dan Cathy.

Truett Cathy and Steve at Truett's last Chick-fil-A Peach Bowl coin toss featuring LSU vs. Clemson, 2012.

One of Stan Richard's famous stairwell meetings at The Richards Group. Stan is standing at the rail.

Truett and Jeanette Cathy in front of the WinShape Center, 2010.

Truett fully embraced the first year of the Cows campaign and the Chick-fil-A Peach Bowl (1996–97). Neither would have happened without his support.

Truett Cathy loved to bring a smile to others, especially customers, so he gave out Chick-fil-A plush cows everywhere he went.

EIGHT

Transitions

Truett turned eighty years old in March 2001 and requested that his birthday party at the home office be catered by the Varsity drive-in. The Varsity is still an institution in Atlanta, serving thousands of customers every day. Its founder, Frank Gordy, was a marketplace disruptor in 1928, creating a drive-in restaurant just as Atlanta was becoming an automobile-centric city.

Imagine . . . the founder of a fast-food restaurant chain filling the home office with the sights, smells, and tastes of a competing brand. Chick-fil-A employees and invited guests chowed down on chili dogs and fries instead of Truett's own creation.

Truett had lived in a nearby housing project as a teenager in the 1930s, and he often walked over to the Varsity, where Mr. Gordy might be in the parking lot directing traffic or inside the restaurant in front of the counter, greeting customers. Decades later, Truett would reference Mr. Gordy's attention to customers as a model for him and Chick-fil-A. The Cathy and Gordy families became friends.

One morning shortly after his eightieth birthday celebration,

Truett joined our executive committee meeting. At that point in his career, Truett was less involved in the day-to-day operations, spending more of his time with the activities of the WinShape Foundation. And on that particular morning, we were already well into the meeting when he stepped into the room and took his place at the head of the table.

Jimmy, who presided over the meetings, asked, "Truett, do you have anything on your mind?"

"Yes," he said. "I've decided that somebody who is eighty years old shouldn't have almost $250 million in debt."

We all chuckled and waited for Truett to tell us what was *really* on his mind. "No," he said, "I'm serious. I want to know how you're going to get me out of debt."

Now, I'm not a finance professional, but the executive committee spent enough time reviewing numbers over the years for me to know that a healthy, growing company whose debt equals less than a quarter of the previous year's sales would be considered a very conservative borrower. Yes, the absolute number sounded huge, but we had more than a thousand restaurants in 2001. We were building and opening fifty to sixty new restaurants every year. That alone required more than $150 million annually. And when we utilized debt, it was only for land and building shells—appreciating assets. As a result, we were still using predominantly cash flow to grow.

None of that was a comfort to Truett. A child of the Depression, to him any debt was a burden. Nineteen years earlier, in 1982, as I have written, we faced a financial crisis that had Truett concerned for the future of the company. And through the years he had often said he could handle any problem except a financial problem. But this was not a problem, and certainly not a crisis.

The Fed Funds Rate had already dropped a point and a half in three months and by the end of 2001 would fall from 6 percent all the way to 1.75 percent. In other words, money was cheaper than at any time in the history of the company. The traditional thinkers then and now would insist that we take advantage of the opportunity to borrow more, not less. With such low interest rates, we could open more stores faster.

Truett was suggesting instead that we finance growth and simultaneously eliminate debt using only cash flow. And he made it clear that this would be one of those few times—I can count all of them on one hand—that he would use his majority vote of one as owner of the company. There was no need for a show of hands.

Buck McCabe, our CFO, and his team went to work on the numbers, and at our next meeting he reported that we could eliminate debt over two or three time-frame scenarios. The greatest impact would be to limit the number of new restaurants we would be able to open.

Truett said the time frames were too long. "I'd like to be alive when we're out of debt," he said.

So Buck and his team sharpened their pencils and came back with a new proposal to eliminate all debt within ten years. But it would cost Chick-fil-A significantly in terms of growth. He had earlier projected that we would reach $5 billion in sales with normal growth and borrowing over that period. If we ceased additional borrowing and eliminated all debt, we would likely reach $3.5 billion in gross sales over the same ten years.

That was fine with Truett.

Year by year the wisdom of Truett's decision grew clearer. Eliminating debt and relying on profits and cash flow for growth made us less likely to outgrow our infrastructure. It's not uncommon for a fast-growing company to borrow money or sell stock, and then two or three years later be in trouble because it grew faster than its infrastructure could support. The company may lack appropriate technology or enough of the right people or adequate systems to maintain quality control. With an influx of cash from borrowing or stock sales, it can ramp up growth and then lose control of the brand because of its inability to support that growth. In our industry, Boston Market and D'Lites had already provided lessons for us.

Truett also understood that without debt, he had more flexibility to invest in the business or to give it away. He always wanted to be flexible when an unexpected opportunity presented itself or if the Holy Spirit led him to invest in a particular ministry. Debt limited that flexibility. This principle is a key component of stewardship. Truett could not be a good steward of all that God had entrusted to him if a bank controlled a portion of it, because it still had to be paid back.

In 2011, Truett would tell the *Atlanta Journal-Constitution*, "In the Great Depression, you bought something if you had the cash to buy it. We are just about debt-free right now, stretching that dollar as far as it will go. If you have debt, you have to worry about it. I would challenge each of you to try to be debt-free."

And in 2012, Dan Cathy announced at the annual Chick-fil-A Operator seminar that the company had achieved its goal and was debt-free. Even the line of credit had been eliminated.

Transitioning to a New Leadership Model

For several years, the executive committee prepared for Jimmy Collins's retirement as president in 2001. Dan Cathy would become president. In that time of preparation, we transitioned at Dan's urging from a model of a single leader to a peer-group accountability team. We planned together, budgeted together, and discussed most significant issues in the business or the culture of the business together. If we could not reach consensus, we thought about it and prayed about it until we could reach an agreement. If someone ultimately had to make a decision, Dan did that. And though Dan was president and chief operating officer, Truett remained the chairman and chief executive officer of Chick-fil-A.

I absorbed the role of facilitating strategic planning for the company from Jimmy, working with the entire executive committee on key planning decisions. My role was to make sure the strategic plan incorporated all the major initiatives from every department that helped us fulfill our purpose and goals. At the right point, the executive committee heard the entire plan and budget, weighed in on it, and then approved it. This revised executive committee team structure and process remained in place until Truett's passing (2014), at which point, Dan Cathy became CEO and built the team to complement his leadership style and goals.

NINE

"My Pleasure"

At the 2001 annual Chick-fil-A Operators seminar, Truett stood in front of all nine hundred restaurant Operators along with their spouses and most of the home office staff and made a request that would transform Chick-fil-A.

He began by telling a story about a trip to a Ritz-Carlton Hotel. He told the audience that when he thanked someone for their assistance, the employee would smile and respond, "My pleasure."

Truett liked the sound of that and the connection he felt with the person who helped him. He shared those two words and how the accompanying smile stayed in his thoughts for days. It was a nice way of telling someone that you were pleased to serve them.

Then he challenged Operators to respond with "my pleasure" instead of "you're welcome" or "no problem" whenever a customer thanked them. Let people know we enjoyed serving them. He believed those two words, *my pleasure*, would remind us and our customers that we really did take pleasure in serving. "You can't say 'my pleasure' without looking them in the eye," he said, and eye contact leads to a personal connection.

I wish I could say we all immediately took up the call. A few Operators accepted Truett's challenge, but most of them, as well as those of us in the home office, didn't give it serious thought.

Operators work under enormous operational pressure, and I could feel their body language saying, *Do you really want me to do these touchy-feely things, all these personal connection things? I'm trying to turn and burn, baby. I'm trying to get the orders accurate, bagged, and out the door, or get them through the drive-thru. You want me to do what? How is that going to drive my sales?*

Truett reminded them, "People come to restaurants even when they're not hungry. They just want the experience."

A year later, at our 2002 Operator seminar, Truett renewed his request for "my pleasure," and a few more Operators put it into practice. Finally, in 2003, Truett's son Dan realized how serious Truett was, and he began to incorporate the phrase into his own vocabulary while encouraging others to do the same. "As I began to incorporate that phrase and that attitude into my vocabulary," Dan said, "it dawned on me that this could be a service signature for us, almost like two pickles on a sandwich. If it could be that consistent across the chain, then it would make a tremendous impact on customers."

In the Chick-fil-A annual message that year, Truett and Dan cowrote a leadership message titled, "My Pleasure":

> "My Pleasure" is more than just an operating standard and more than just a personal request. "My Pleasure" is an expression from the heart where team members, Operators, or staff members literally show that they want to go the extra mile—that they truly care about the other person. They have enough value in the other person to exceed expectations.

It was a transformative moment for Chick-fil-A that would strengthen our "Blue Ocean Strategy" space—that place where we were operating without competition or where competition was irrelevant. Truett (and Dan) Cathy, with the simple challenge to say "my pleasure," was charting a course to a place where a warm greeting would infuse every Chick-fil-A restaurant and create a culture of genuine hospitality (more on this to come).

Another journey was about to begin.

Raving Fans Camping Out in Phoenix

Later in 2003, Dan experienced another personal-connection marketing event in Phoenix, Arizona, that would reveal to all of us the potential power of the Chick-fil-A brand to be really different.

We were opening our first freestanding restaurant in Phoenix after a few openings in California. As was our style, we were moving conservatively into new markets out West. Dan arrived on Wednesday morning for the Thursday morning opening. The prior week, one of our marketing associates, Tiffany Holland, who was already in Phoenix helping on preparations, had called Barry White in our department with an idea that might generate some publicity. Why not give away free Chick-fil-A for a year—fifty-two Be Our Guest cards for combo meals—to the first one hundred customers? Barry loved the idea, shared it with David Salyers, and when they brought it to me, I told them to go for it.

Tiffany was smart, aggressive, and good at buttoning down details. We were confident she could pull it off. So when Dan arrived the day before the grand opening, she told him about the idea. A little skeptical, Dan asked how it would work. He also wondered how people would know about the promotion. Tiffany explained that she had already gotten some good PR coverage through local radio, TV, and newspapers, including a local radio station partner. He liked that.

Tiffany walked away to take care of something, and about that time a man drove into the parking lot and asked Dan where the line started.

Dan said there wasn't a line. The restaurant wasn't open yet. He should come back on Thursday.

The man explained he had heard about the first one hundred customers promotion, and he didn't want to miss it. He was going to stay all night.

Dan was giddy that a customer would be so determined and also concerned that the man would be sleeping in the parking lot alone all night. Moments later a woman arrived with a lawn chair, clearly intending to wait in what was now officially a line, and by nightfall a dozen more people arrived.

Nobody had taken this possibility into account. Dan found the store Operator and suggested he have somebody stay with the restaurant through the night so they could make sure everybody was safe and let the campers have access to the bathrooms.

At sunrise on Thursday morning, a news helicopter was circling overhead with the anchor reporting on live television, showing images of tents, lawn chairs, and more than a hundred customers waiting in line. Another local TV reporter arrived and interviewed some of the overnight campers for his morning news show. "Why would you stay out here all night long? How did you know about Chick-fil-A? It's new to Phoenix."

The answers were powerful, and the public relations impact exceeded anything we could have imagined. We counted up the coverage and realized we had received the equivalent of six figures' worth of stories on TV, radio, and newspapers, not to mention social media from the campers themselves. Those campers suggested to us that the brand reached much deeper and wider into America than we knew, emotionally and personally.

Dan was meeting Chick-fil-A Raving Fans, and he believed they could play a crucial role in the future of the brand. He came back to the home office and described what he had seen, adding that the "First 100" must become a brand signature event at all Chick-fil-A grand openings. We certainly agreed with him.

This was a strategic store-opening shift in strategy that I strongly advocated. The history of Chick-fil-A had been to have "normal day" new-store openings (not too aggressive). The assumption was that the operational pressure of opening a new restaurant was difficult enough without generating large crowds. Another assumption was that sales would grow over time.

The data showed, however, that during the first three years, a new store's strongest months would be the first three. More importantly, the data showed that the stronger the sales in the first three months, the healthier the sales long term. If we could maximize our grand opening traffic, the store could take advantage of all that activity, free publicity, and early customer trial to create momentum into the future.

The pushback: How do we prepare Operators and team members to serve two or three times the "normal day" customer traffic during their *first ninety days in business*?

Tiffany Holland's initiative forced that conversation. We decided that we would continue with the First 100 promotion, opening new stores not just on the strength of the brand, but with rockets and flares declaring, "We are here! Not just in your city, but at this site!"

We sent operations and marketing teams to restaurants weeks in advance to help develop and orchestrate the grand opening plans. They helped select and train team members, gave away Chick-fil-A samples and Be Our Guest cards, and found other marketing opportunities.

We sent media professionals to reach out to the community. And we sent in the Cows.

We now had to be ready for a big crowd the minute we opened the door, and that required a completely different level of staffing and training. There was no three-week ramp-up after a soft opening. From 6:00 a.m. on opening day, the whole thing was on steroids.

Raving Fan Strategy

The Phoenix experience with the *first* First 100 also stimulated our thinking about ways to identify and create more Raving Fans, a distinction that our friend Ken Blanchard embraced in his book *Raving Fans: A Revolutionary Approach to Customer Service.*

We began studying great contemporary brands and discovered common traits among their fans. If you build a great brand, three good outcomes occur:

- People will come more often.
- They'll pay full price, because you're delivering value beyond just the functional benefits.
- They'll tell others about their experience with your brand.

By the way, they'll not just tell others about how good their experience was; they'll tell you if you've disappointed them, because they care that much.

Fred Reichheld, *New York Times* bestselling author and a business strategist with Bain & Company, helped guide us on that final descriptor of Raving Fans (telling others). Fred, who was named by the *Economist* "the high priest of loyalty," based his book *The Ultimate Question: Driving Good Profits and True Growth* on the fact that customer satisfaction can ultimately be measured by the question, "Would you recommend this business to a friend based on your experience today?" We surveyed customers and noted their answers on a scale of 1 to 10, with 1 being a definite no and 10 being a definite yes. We categorized only those who gave us a 10 as Raving Fans—customers who most likely exhibited the three behaviors I mentioned above.

We knew Chick-fil-A had Raving Fans, because we had seen them. I had been calling them Brand Ambassadors. Could we develop a strategy that would create more Raving Fans? Every day, at every Chick-fil-A, not just at grand openings?

We reviewed our history and our current strengths and recognized three broad strategic categories of activities we had developed over the years that, all working together at a location, created Raving Fans:

- Executing Operational Excellence
- Delivering Second-Mile Service
- Activating Emotional Connections Marketing

Operational Excellence

Truett and Jimmy had insisted on operational excellence from the first day that the first Chick-fil-A restaurant opened. Then Truett had triggered our thinking toward Second-Mile Service with his request for "my pleasure." And the Cows and personal engagement of our people and food had opened our eyes to the power of marketing that emotionally connected with our customers.

Building a comprehensive strategy around all three could amplify the power of each.

Operational excellence begins with the food. Truett opened his first Chick-fil-A restaurant in 1967 after other restaurants that had agreed to serve his new sandwich could not deliver the quality product he demanded. Fifty years after the first mall restaurant opened,

Chick-fil-A still begins with fresh ingredients to serve crave-able food. The business has always been focused on fresh food and has consistently continued to improve on operational excellence. This was our first mile. It was the foundation the chain built its reputation on. You cannot deliver Second-Mile Service and have it be credible if there's something wrong with the first mile: the food, the fundamental interaction with staff, the cleanliness, speed, or accuracy. It's got to be right, or hospitality lacks credibility. This is the traditional focus of any restaurant, and Chick-fil-A strives to do it better than the others.

Second-Mile Service

As Truett and Dan wrote in their 2003 message to the Chick-fil-A family, "my pleasure" was an expression of the heart. That expression became the inspiration for Second-Mile Service throughout the Chick-fil-A chain.

Dan personally took the challenge to develop a model for hospitality by first helping define the opportunity. He looked into the origins of the phrase "go the second mile," which appears in the Bible in Matthew 5:41. Jesus told His disciples, "If anyone forces you to go one mile, go with them two miles" (NIV). This was in the context of Jesus telling them to "love your enemies" and to "turn the other cheek."

In those days of Roman occupation of Palestine, the law allowed a Roman soldier to compel a Jew to carry his pack for one mile, but no farther. Those forced into temporary servitude surely counted their steps and put down the pack as soon as they were legally allowed. Now this Jewish preacher was telling them to carry the soldier's load a second mile as an act of kindness. The voluntary service could transform both the soldier and the servant by raising the obvious question—"Why would you do that?"—thus giving the follower of Christ an opportunity to share why he would see and serve the soldier as one of

God's creations. Why not treat all people who step into Chick-fil-A the same way, with honor, dignity, and respect? An unexpected second mile?

Dan then reached out to the Ritz-Carlton, which had been Truett's inspiration. Aspiring brands learn from great brands, and in the hospitality industry there may not be a better brand than Ritz-Carlton. The Hôtel Ritz opened in Paris in 1898 and immediately earned a reputation for luxury, offering bathrooms *en suite*, telephones, and electricity in every room. Owner César Ritz was called "hotelier to kings and king of hoteliers" by Edward VII, who was a regular guest at Ritz's Carlton Hotel in London. And when Irving Berlin wrote "Puttin' on the Ritz" in 1929, he was simply putting into song the Ritz's well-earned reputation for glamour.

Decades later, however, the Ritz brand had diminished worldwide. Atlantan William B. Johnson bought the brand for $75 million in 1983 and assembled a team of professionals led by Horst Schulze, previously general manager and vice president of Hyatt Hotels, to give it new life. Schulze became chief operating officer of the company, which built thirty hotels across the globe in ten years. He coined the phrase: "We are ladies and gentlemen serving ladies and gentlemen." For its commitment to customer service, Ritz-Carlton twice won the prestigious Malcolm Baldrige National Quality Award, presented by the United States Department of Commerce.

We pursued an opportunity to learn from the best. Ritz-Carlton was headquartered in Atlanta, making it convenient for Horst Schulze to meet with several of our staff and Operators. He was very familiar with Chick-fil-A, and he understood our category. Standing in front of us, he drew a box with three different levels of restaurant service inside. At the top he wrote the names of fine-dining restaurants like the Dining Room at the Ritz-Carlton, Atlanta's only five-star restaurant at the time. In the second tier he included full-service and family-style restaurants like Applebee's and Longhorn Steakhouse. Below those, in the bottom section, were fast-food restaurants.

Horst wrote "Chick-fil-A" near the top of the fast-food section. "You're the best of a bad lot," he told us. "The best of the worst. If you're going to have a vision of an exciting and uplifting organization, then over time you need to break out of that box—redefine who you want to be as a business and the kind of experience you want your guests to have." But, how?

"Don't look to be better than the other fast-food restaurants," Horst told us. "Those limited expectations will just weigh you down. Instead, aspire to the next level of service—restaurants with price points that are at least double Chick-fil-A's, and build a service model that resembles those." There was a space in the marketplace, he explained, that was neither fast-food nor casual dining—a space that Chick-fil-A could own exclusively. He was describing our Blue Ocean Strategy before the book had been written.

In that moment, as we considered the possibilities, those of us in the room suddenly felt as if we had been released—set free to create an entirely new service model without the constraints of the fast-food tradition. Intrigued with this idea, we began to study Houston's, Macaroni Grill, and other restaurants that were three times our price point, to see the service elements that made people feel good about spending fifteen or twenty dollars for a meal. Then we considered which of those elements we could incorporate into the Chick-fil-A dining experience.

Though the transformation would touch every corner of Chick-fil-A, from restaurants to the corporate staff, we led the initiative from the marketing department, assigning leadership to Mark Moraitakis. He became our director of hospitality and service design. His primary charter: How do we develop a consistent hospitality model, keeping the Chick-fil-A customer central during this service innovation journey?

Rather than decide what *we* liked, Mark and his team asked

customers about *their* expectations for service at Chick-fil-A. He also tested ideas that Operators were already utilizing in their restaurants, such as fresh flowers on the tables, umbrellas at the door on rainy days, and a pepper grinder on the condiments table.

"Of all the ideas we're piloting in stores," we asked customers, "which made you feel most cared for? Which ones made you want to come back to Chick-fil-A?"

More than 90 percent of guests answered, "When someone smiles at me, looks me in the eye, and lets me know I'm being cared for and treated with excellence. That's above and beyond what I expect at a fast-food restaurant." Really!

Most of our Operators had been encouraging those behaviors for decades, but they were not 100 percent predictable. Whether they were getting lost among the list of other requests or team members simply forgot, a smile, a warm greeting, and eye contact were not happening every time, everywhere. (Remember Truett at that early store opening?)

If these were the desires of our guests, then we needed to package them in a way that made them easy for team members to remember and practice. So we created the Core 4:

- Create eye contact.
- Share a smile.
- Speak with an enthusiastic tone.
- Stay connected to make it personal.

These were the four behaviors we wanted team members to extend whenever they were engaging a guest in a restaurant. When we packaged the request that way, it was amazing to see how teachable it was. Team members got it. The requirements were not lost among the other requirements in the quality guide.

In addition to Horst, our hospitality team reached out to Danny

Meyer, whose Union Square Hospitality Group owned such iconic white-tablecloth restaurants as Gramercy Tavern, renowned for a culture of "Enlightened Hospitality." (Danny later opened Shake Shack in 2004.)

Danny helped us understand that *service* is the way you deliver the meal—the presentation, the consistency, the quality. *Hospitality* is how you add value after the meal has been delivered—the second mile. Hospitality goes beyond just successfully, accurately, personably delivering the meal and adds connection.

Hospitality adds unexpected surprises like refreshing a drink or giving a surprise dessert while guests are enjoying their meal. These steps might represent the expected level of service at an upscale restaurant. But at a fast-food restaurant, they become unexpected hospitality, letting guests know how much they are appreciated.

And unlike Ritz-Carlton, where the goal is elegance, Horst suggested visitors to Chick-fil-A should experience cheerfulness with every visit.

"Cheerfulness extended from warm hearts," he said. "Don't get too formal. Remember, you're in the fast-food industry. You have to bring genuine cheerfulness and warm hearts into the service element. Otherwise, it's only about the food, and you cannot thrive if the transaction is only about food." He was helping us learn another way to become endearing, not just functionally sound.

We benchmarked other companies outside our industry that had high levels of operational consistency and great service reputations with customers—Disney, Apple, Harley-Davidson, Southwest Airlines, Zappos, and others. We visited several of those companies' headquarters and sought to understand their philosophy about service—what kind of infrastructure did they create to replicate hospitality? (It seems counterintuitive to "institutionalize" hospitality, and yet people need the right tools for consistent expression.) Then we envisioned how we might train those standards in our environment.

We didn't want to stop at "smiling and eye contact" and "my pleasure," so we explored what we might add to take us into the second mile, and we selected three additional behaviors:

- Carry eat-in meals to the table.
- Check in with guests for any needs.
- Carry large orders, such as Chick-fil-A trays, to the car.

These simple, proactive behaviors became our "recipe for service." As the name implies, this recipe consists of ingredients that are as critical as the ingredients in any of our menu items.

Training the entire chain on these new behaviors, we believed, would work best at regional off-site locations. Mark's team, however, suggested that training might be more memorable and impactful in actual restaurants. We agreed and selected nine restaurants in our Atlantic region to pilot the training.

The team brought in professionals to serve as external consultants to the Operators of those nine restaurants: Peter Goode, an effective "edutrainer," and Rod Stoner, retired thirty-year head of food services for the Greenbrier Resort. Rod and Peter coached the Operators and their teams to become Second-Mile Service experts—models for all the other restaurants in the region. They went to those nine restaurants twice a month, teaching and listening. We had never offered that level of intensity in training at Chick-fil-A.

After months of preparation, we trained our first regional group of team members in a restaurant. That morning a rainstorm hit, and the food truck was late with its delivery to one of the restaurants, diminishing the quality of that learning environment. "I had been in the restaurant the previous week," Mark Moraitakis recalled, "and it was an unbelievably good experience. Everybody was living Second-Mile Service. The problems we saw the day of training weren't a reflection of the Operator or the team. They were a reflection of the pace of our business. We learned that our restaurants are the ideal places to serve our guests, but they might not offer the ideal environment to teach specific new behaviors."

Mark and the team walked out of the restaurant that day knowing that training would have to be focused and centralized, and they wondered how to create a controlled environment that could still reflect the realities of our business. We needed a "training camp."

Coincidentally, back in Atlanta, our Chick-fil-A University was in the process of building a full-size replica of a restaurant in a warehouse near our corporate headquarters so they could train new Operators and create materials and product photography in a more controlled environment. We investigated the possibility of training all our Operators in that simulator, but the numbers didn't work. We would need two simulators to train everyone in a timely fashion.

We built a second simulator, complete with a drive-thru window and electric golf carts for drive-thru "customers." To make the experience as realistic as possible, we recruited customers to come into the simulators, role play, then offer their feedback. We trained more than two thousand leaders—an Operator and another leader from each restaurant—then sent them home to train their teams.

The hospitality team had started with *my pleasure*, two words Truett had shared with us seven years earlier—two words that would unleash the most powerful branding tool ever: the hearts of Chick-fil-A Operators and their team members.

Emotional Connections Marketing

And how about the third leg of the Raving Fan Strategy? Since 1946, Truett had created emotional connections by making friends with customers, giving away food, and extending his heart in countless other ways. Half a century later, the Chick-fil-A Cows were making a different kind of emotional connection, making people laugh. How could we expand and boost the process of making emotional connections? How could we equip Operators to prepare their team members to be proactive brand ambassadors—to come out from behind the counter and create new guest experiences in the restaurants and the community?

Relying on Operators to continue building the brand and sales, we focused on four marketing assets that they could leverage better than our competition—assets *only* available to Chick-fil-A Operators:

- Our food
- Our people
- The Cows
- Their influence in their communities

Our Food

We started with food, which we too often underestimated and underutilized. As I've said, since the earliest days of the original Dwarf House, Truett had been giving away food, especially during difficult times such as illness or death. That was Truett's way of being a neighbor. Then when the first Chick-fil-A restaurant opened in 1967, Truett and his family stood at the lease line, where the restaurant opened into the mall, offering samples of Chick-fil-A on toothpicks. They were introducing a brand-new food product, and the response was instant.

Though we gave away literally millions of Be Our Guest cards (BOGs) over the years for free Chick-fil-A sandwiches, we believed those cards still lacked the power of real food. To confirm that belief, in conjunction with a grand opening, we blitzed a community with ten thousand BOGs. At the same time, we gave away ten thousand free sandwiches with an accompanying BOG. The redemption rate on the cards with accompanying sandwiches was two and a half times greater than the redemption rate of the cards alone.

Restaurants often give away samples of new products they're introducing or to energize sales for an existing product. In Houston, for example, Operators throughout the market pooled their resources and for one day a week over a six-week period gave away eight hundred breakfast samples per restaurant. This wasn't a buy-one-get-one kind of deal. The food was a flat-out gift. People love our food, and when we give it to them, they connect a pleasurable experience with someone at Chick-fil-A being generous. By the end of the event, Houston restaurants had doubled their breakfast sales.

We had three primary goals when we were sampling: introduce the product, remind people of Chick-fil-A, and reinforce a spirit of generosity. We wanted people to know that we cared enough about them to give them food with no strings attached. Nothing to redeem. Just free food. Almost everywhere else you look in the industry, if it's "free," it has a string attached. Truett had a complete, unabashed spirit of generosity. Why wouldn't we want that to migrate and grow throughout the entire chain?

It's not uncommon for Operators to give away as much as 1 percent of their sales in free food. They're casting their bread on the water, and it always comes back. Or it's like the principle of the harvest: you reap what you sow, and more than you sow. There's an emotional payoff that comes with being generous with no strings attached.

And like Truett since 1946, Operators responded to difficult situations large and small with food, every day, all across the chain. Two high-profile Atlanta examples occurred during the time that I was writing this book: When a fire shut down a major interstate, Operators responded with free food for first responders. When the interstate was closed for months, the city asked commuters to help reduce traffic by carpooling. Operators encouraged and rewarded the effort by offering free breakfast entrees to carpoolers. Then on a Sunday in December 2017, when Hartsfield–Jackson International Airport was shut down for hours because of a power failure, Atlanta Mayor Kasim Reed called Dan Cathy at 10:00 p.m. and asked for help. Staff and team members who lived near the airport immediately mobilized and delivered more than five thousand free sandwiches and bottled water to stranded passengers.

These were examples that garnered nationwide attention. Most of the time, though, we share food person-to-person with a simple smile.

Our People

Leveraging our people was a matter of equipping them to do what they do best: interact with customers. Chick-fil-A Operators attracted a high caliber of team members who, because of their personalities, often had a natural hospitality or marketing bent. Putting them out in the dining room, the drive-thru, or engaging directly with folks in the community, transformed a transaction into a relationship.

Another high-profile example occurred in Houston in the wake of Hurricane Harvey. An elderly couple was trapped in their home by rising waters and called 911. When they couldn't get a response, they called the next best thing: their favorite Chick-fil-A location.

"I ordered two grilled chicken burritos with extra egg and a boat," J. C. Spencer told *Good Morning America*. "And can you believe that one of the managers of Chick-fil-A, she sent her husband to pick us up (in a boat), and we are so grateful."[8]

Mr. and Mrs. Spencer were regular customers, and restaurant general manager Jeffrey Urban recognized the number when they called. He contacted a coworker, who called her husband, who took his boat to rescue the Spencers.

It's more typical for a team member to help a customer with an umbrella in a rainstorm or a drink refresh, but we enjoy telling the stories of the heroic acts that build relationships as well.

The Cows

By many measures, the Chick-fil-A Cows make their own unique emotional connections. For example, the Cow calendar has historically been the number one selling calendar in the world, even outselling the *Sports Illustrated* swimsuit edition! People hung calendars on the walls in millions of homes, offices, and school lockers, bringing the Chick-fil-A brand into their personal spaces. Every day of the year, they were inviting the Cows to give them a smile and remind them to "Eat Mor Chikin."

The Cows moved from an advertising campaign to an unexpectedly fun connecting point for customers. They showed up at football games, small-town parades, and in the restaurants themselves, and they were absolute rock stars. They sometimes visited children's hospitals with football players and other human celebrities, and the kids immediately lit up. The kids didn't ignore the celebrities, but it was the Cows that they wanted a picture with. Operators sometimes have to remind themselves how special the Cows are. They can't let the fact that the Cows are around so often blind them to their power. They help maintain the Cows' celebrity status by keeping them in the limelight, on billboards, TV, radio, and local events. People love the Cows, and only Chick-fil-A has them, so we share them.

Community Influence

Influence lies at the heart of the Chick-fil-A corporate purpose: "to have a positive influence on all who come in contact with Chick-fil-A."

Part of the beauty of the Operator concept is that the Operator typically stays at the same restaurant for many years—often for decades. So those Operators have a vested interest in the community because they live there. They're raising their own families there. As a result, they grow attached to the people who live in their community.

It's a natural response. The store gives the Operator a platform to serve the community, starting with their team members.

Neighbors then become more endeared to the brand because of that relationship. That's not why Truett did what he did, and it's not why Operators do what they do, but it's that cultural soil that they help create, work in, and live in. The business was designed to engage with people locally and to have an influence in the community.

Counting Raving Fans

We asked customers in every Chick-fil-A restaurant in the country if they would recommend Chick-fil-A to a friend based on their experience. As I mentioned earlier, the only answer that *guaranteed* the customer was categorized as a Chick-fil-A Raving Fan was 10. Not a 9, and certainly not an 8. People who answered 10 were the strongest marketing advocates of the business. Over time we learned how many Raving Fans each restaurant had. Not surprisingly, success and growth of individual restaurants corresponded closely with the number of Raving Fans. Then the collaborative culture of the chain encouraged the sharing of ideas among Operators on how to create more. Along the way, we learned and applied some key principles.

Four Habits That Fuel the Execution of the Raving Fans Strategy

Focus on Giving, not Getting

It's not how much we give but *how* we give that's important. When we give to friends and family, it looks like a wrapped box. But sometimes when we give through business, it looks like strings attached. This is not a gift. It's a trade. If we expect something in return, it's not a gift. This creates transactions. We'll take all the transactions we can get, but when it comes to creating Raving Fans, it doesn't start with thinking of transaction. It starts with interaction.

What we need to give is not a discount. Sometimes it's not even free food. Rather, we give the gift of knowing a customer's name and a smile—the gift of valuing the customer as a person.

Focus on Remarkable, not Ordinary

People don't remark about the ordinary. Word-of-mouth advertising is the most powerful marketing anywhere. To earn it, we must be doing things worth talking about. We can't just provide a product; we must provide an experience. What will they remember about the experience? What will they talk about? Are we creating and giving *remarkable* experiences? Chick-fil-A can be far more than a meal. It must be an experience.

Focus on the Emotional, not Just the Rational

Rational generates transactions. Emotional creates Raving Fans. A rational developer of toys for kids' meals wonders what kind of gimmick will attract a child. At Chick-fil-A, we asked how we could use our Kid's Meal to create an emotional connection between a parent and a child. How could we have positive influences on children?

Businesses focused on emotional connections use their platforms to make a meaningful impact on customers. Then those customers become more supportive of the business. They actually root for its success and feel obligated to do business there. Do things worth rooting for. Do things for customers that can't be weighed or measured—that aren't expected.

The destination with the customer is what's important, not

whether you can count and measure all the steps to get there. Raving Fans can be counted on to come in without a coupon or deal and pay full price, and they feel good about it. That makes a business more sustainable.

Focus on Active, not Passive

Great relationships require passion, and passion needs to be refilled. If you've ever seen a Chick-fil-A grand opening, you've seen passion. Passionate customers camping out all night waiting for the doors to open. Passionate Operators and team members connecting with those customers in the parking lot and excited to serve them on opening morning.

Operators and team members connect with passion when they move through the dining room alert to opportunities to serve. They greet customers, deliver orders to tables, refresh drinks, and clear tables. They take large orders to cars and offer an umbrella on rainy days. And they always respond with "my pleasure" when they are thanked, whether at the counter or in the drive-thru.

TEN

Innovation

The brand IS the business.

This is not a new concept, but it was new to Chick-fil-A in the 1980s. Corporate leadership believed "the brand" was the domain of the marketing department. Whatever we did with marketing, advertising, and public relations constituted the brand. In reality, the brand is the totality of the customer experience with the business.

Everything the customer sees and touches shapes the brand: the menu, store design, cleanliness of the bathroom, packaging, advertising, promotions, team members, and even their apparel are all part of the brand. Any customer touchpoint shapes the brand, and it either adds value to the brand or denigrates it.

About ten years ago we committed to put on paper the Chick-fil-A brand architecture, allowing anyone to see at a glance the entire system of these "brand touchpoints" interactions and how they fit together and how they should drive our innovation priorities.

It started with the corporate purpose—why we existed. Then, our mission, "Be REMARKable." We wanted every brand encounter to be remarkable. A key to our success was that customers talked about us in a positive way. To inspire those positive remarks, we offered the unexpected, so they were surprised. We did that through finding ways to express our brand essence: "Where good meets gracious."

We illustrated the brand touchpoints around a wheel with the brand essence at the center, because if you lay that wheel on top of an organizational structure, you can't have any functional silos. Everyone has to work around the wheel. All around the circle, even if marketing does not have direct accountability, marketing has influence in the work. And specifically, every noted brand touchpoint has a cross-function team working on it: its plan, budget, and execution.

Marketing's first line of influence was supporting the Operator, who was serving the customer—and not just the customer's tangible, functional product experience. The Operator was reinforcing the feeling that, yes, Chick-fil-A delivered well, and they did it with grace today. Not only inside the restaurant, but in the drive-thru, or over at that baseball game, or in that office catering event. We delivered "where good meets gracious" in whatever environment the customer was in.

We didn't look at customers as, "Oh, we have two thousand customers a day going through a particular store." No, we've got two thousand people choosing to visit that store. They each have their own issues, problems, challenges—they each have their own story. They're in the midst of a story at the very moment they encounter Chick-fil-A. Now, how did we impact their story? How did we deliver "where good meets gracious"? How did we help make their story today better? Quite frankly, they may not be having a very good day, and Chick-fil-A has the potential to help change the script.

The home office supported Operators with a brand strategy and brand architecture, and also with all the infrastructure services that allowed them to focus on delivering the brand. They couldn't focus on delivering and building the Chick-fil-A brand if they were worried about their IT systems or accounting or whether the next delivery would come on time. All those things had to work in order for them to focus on the customer. (For further details, see brand architecture and brand touchpoints circle in the photo insert, pages 5–6.)

Remembering Our "Why"

By the summer of 2012, Truett had been demonstrating to me for more than thirty years that he wanted to build a relationship with every customer—to earn their business and their respect. His sensitivity and his desire to please others was paramount. He avoided social, political, and religious activism because he knew those things divided relationships. On the other hand, everybody enjoys good food and being cared for.

Of course, Truett had opinions and beliefs, but he had chosen not to use his business as a platform for those.

In 2012, we experienced a public relations crisis that drove us back to our "why." Why does Chick-fil-A exist? When we had debated the words of the corporate purpose in 1982, there had been extensive discussion about how best to glorify God. That was an undeniable desire on the part of Truett, Dan, and Bubba Cathy, and members of the executive team. That led to the "how": by being faithful stewards of *all* God entrusted to the business.

Truett wanted a business that had a God-honoring testimony visible through being good stewards of people, money, and influence. Ultimately, as his favorite verse, Proverbs 22:1, reminded us, reputation is more important than any earthly riches. While discussing this point, Truett told his young team that he saw Chick-fil-A as a powerful testimony on how to treat and serve others, and he wanted to do that on the largest platform possible. As a part of this goal, he made it clear he did not desire Chick-fil-A to be a platform for social, political, or religious narratives or positions. I heard him reiterate this point many times through the years.

He operated a business that served anyone and everyone—"have a positive influence on *all* who come in contact with Chick-fil-A"—in a way that might cause people to recognize a distinctive difference in their Chick-fil-A experience, and might even cause people to ask, "What makes Chick-fil-A different?" By serving everyone, he and the executive committee hoped to earn a place of good reputation and influence in their lives, allowing the local Operators to address the "why."

In 2012, when Chick-fil-A stood in the middle of a cultural debate, we did not want to water down what the Cathy family believed, yet we wanted to be faithful to the "why" of our corporate purpose of honoring God by "having a positive influence on all we touched."

It was an extremely difficult time throughout the Chick-fil-A family. Restaurant Operators and their team members didn't want to be the rope in this tug-of-war. And yet, they could look out the restaurant window and see people on both sides of the debate using Chick-fil-A to further their agendas. And what did they do? The gracious thing. They gave them free sandwiches and lemonade, with no prompting from the home office. Exactly what Truett would have done!

Don Perry and I were trying to manage the social narrative, which too often remained beyond our control. We just wanted to bring us back to a place where Chick-fil-A could have a positive influence on all we touched.

And how did we "touch" people? We could throw out social media or public relations statements from the support center, but the real power of stewardship and positive influence rested in the hands of the more than one thousand Operators in their restaurants, attracting and developing young talent and serving their communities up close and personal. We had always been focused on equipping and supporting them in their Chick-fil-A business. That included an opportunity to serve and influence as many people as possible.

After reflection time and much discussion, we released a brief statement:

> *The Chick-fil-A culture and service tradition in our restaurants is to treat every person with honor, dignity, and respect—regardless of their belief, race, creed, sexual orientation, or gender.*

This crisis turned into a blessing because it forced us back to our past. What in our past was still crucial to our future? We engaged the Prophet consulting group and its founder, Scott Davis, and partner, Mike Fleming, to help us hear from our customers.

The customers reminded us that Operators and their teams brought to life the best of Chick-fil-A. They were our future. They met, greeted, and served people with genuine, caring service. And they extended the spirit of gracious hospitality that Truett had always modeled and preached. He designed the Operator model to re-create that hospitality in every Chick-fil-A location.

Because of the way Operators responded to this crisis, we saw the reality of a business that did genuinely desire to honor God by serving everyone in a way that communicated authentic concern and graciousness. At its core, the Chick-fil-A Corporate Purpose was about being good stewards of God's grace to Truett, his family, and all those who shared his business vision. I am convinced, based on the experience of being in the room when the corporate purpose was written, that this was Truett's heart—his vision and desire. I found it amazingly refreshing and encouraging to be able to join him in that kind of purpose—a clear "why" the business existed and implicitly, as I have highlighted, the embedded principles by which we would lead and make decisions.

The summer of 2012 eventually resulted in a renewed brand clarity. The customer data that Prophet received showed that Chick-fil-A customers believed they owned the brand, something every business dreams of, and it was a significant part of their lives. They said the Chick-fil-A they knew and loved did not align with the descriptions they were reading on social media. "The Chick-fil-A I know is courteous, caring, and offers good food," they said—Operators and their team members at their best!

During a period of months, we were encouraged as we saw Operators continuing to create a place where good meets gracious. Customer feedback gave us those four words, *where good meets gracious*, which we realized were the essence of the Chick-fil-A brand.

- *Where.* Anywhere, not just in a restaurant, but any encounter with the Chick-fil-A brand. "Anywhere I encounter Chick-fil-A, I expect it to be . . ."
- *Good.* Good people, good food, good environment, good service.
- *Meets.* Connections. Eye contact. "My pleasure." And encounters that say Chick-fil-A Operators, team members, employees, and staff genuinely care about you.
- *Gracious.* Gracious hospitality and the personal touches people don't expect, especially in a fast-food restaurant.

Good people, good food, good environment delivered with a spirit of graciousness to all . . . at our restaurants, the events they serve, and those who work there. My confidence level was and remains high that the Chick-fil-A Operator family has and will continue to stay focused on creating those kinds of encounters. They and their teams are the brand. They know and love Chick-fil-A's purpose and know how to gracefully live it out.

In the midst of these events, Don Perry, vice president of public relations, who did everything with a spirit of humility and graciousness, passed away on July 27, 2012. The loss of our good friend was painful. But when his wife, Marilyn, asked me to deliver one of the eulogies, Don's memorial was easy to write because of his character, wonderful personality, and influence. Although I was emotional, it was a joy to share about a man I had grown to love and respect so much. On the same day we celebrated Don's life and legacy, millions of customers were standing in lines at Chick-fil-A locations across America to show their support for Chick-fil-A. It was a challenging day for me—a day when I experienced God's peace among Don's family and loving friends who had packed the church to honor him. A day that reminded me of what is really important—our heavenly and earthly relationships. But it was also a day that reaffirmed my commitment to do all I could to position the reality of Chick-fil-A—a place of graciousness, humility, and hospitality. Truett, the Operators, and Don deserved that.

Innovating to Maintain Brand Relevance

Innovation has always been key to Chick-fil-A's success, beginning with the creation of the sandwich itself. We continued to engage in an ongoing, constantly moving process of change in order to keep the brand relevant. Brand relevance, not just innovation for its own sake, was a top priority of the marketing group—to keep the brand relevant to customers' lifestyles, tastes, and expectations.

Through the decades, we developed and honed a formal process where we systematically listened to customers and Operators as we innovated products, store designs, or hospitality initiatives.

In the menu space alone, innovation led to Chick-fil-A nuggets and soup, waffle fries, and kids' meals with toys that made a positive influence. When customers indicated they wanted us to step up our salad options beyond coleslaw and carrot and raisin salad, we wondered if they would buy a side salad. The answer, they told us very quickly, was yes. The success led us to develop an entire salad lineup.

Encouraged by the nutritional halo of salads, we developed grilled chicken recipes that gave us both sandwich and salad options.

Frank Carney and Shane Todd, veteran Operators in north Georgia, pioneered their own milkshakes, and when we saw the buzz they were creating, we took on the challenge. The new product development team worked to perfect the recipes, coordinating with suppliers to source the ingredients. We started with Frank's and Shane's proven milkshakes and worked on the recipe and procedures. But it was taking too long to prepare a shake. And we were burning up spinners and tearing up cups.

There wasn't equipment on the market that could deliver a milkshake in our packaging fast enough. So our engineering team worked for almost two years to create and produce a mixer that could stand up to the volume and be easy to use in stores. The end result: milkshakes are now a huge part of the Chick-fil-A brand experience.

Even as we were innovating as rapidly as we should and could, the marketplace became more demanding and more competitive, and we had to work harder to maintain our Blue Ocean space. The pace of required innovation demanded shorter cycle times, so under the leadership of David Farmer and a cross-functional team, we created a nearly one-hundred-thousand-square-foot innovation center, which opened in 2012. We named the facility "Hatch." It allowed us to put the entire innovation process under a single roof, with full-size restaurant prototypes, virtual 3-D store design technology, and flexible workspaces. Hatch also allowed us to bring customers and Operators physically into the early stages of the innovation process.

We could brainstorm and get feedback on conceptual ideas, whether they were products, technology, advertisements, menu board layouts, or team member apparel. We got immediate customer feedback. We could prototype store designs, serve food, or exercise hospitality role-playing under the same roof. Before Hatch, the only "live" way to experience customer interaction with new ideas was in actual restaurants—a slower process.

In 2014, we created a separate space dedicated wholly to food, the Kitchen, a thirty-thousand-square-foot facility where we could work on new recipe ideas and improve existing products, procedures, and equipment to make kitchens safer and more efficient.

At any time, we had fifteen or twenty projects going on in Hatch or the Kitchen, suggested by people throughout the organization. No matter their role or position in the business, anyone could champion a great idea for strategic support, team talent allocation, and innovation process funding. Innovation was most often fostered by folks closest to customers and Operators. When creative people worked in a creative environment where everybody around them was focused on innovation, that creativity became contagious.

Another benefit of Hatch and the Kitchen was that all the project leaders were using the same innovative processes. They were all listening to customers and Operators on the front end. Then they took their ideas to their respective desks with pen and pencil, or with computers and CAD systems, or, literally, to the kitchen counter where they experimented with recipes. Sometimes it meant collaborating with a chef to help them think outside the box about menu options.

That's exactly how the Superfood Side Salad (with broccolini and kale) was developed.

Principal results of innovation in Hatch and the Kitchen included processes and equipment to improve food preparation in the restaurants. Chick-fil-A restaurants serve considerably more food every day than other fast-food restaurants, and the equipment must stand up to that volume. And they have to be fast and safe. Truett knew that from the start, when he cut the bone out of the chicken breast and then cooked it in a pressure fryer. He didn't, however, envision the hand preparation of biscuits for breakfast at Chick-fil-A. An example of innovation to simplify processes in the Kitchen: they developed a unique rolling pin that looks like it has biscuit cutters attached so that it can roll across flattened dough and cut twenty biscuits in a single pass.

Customer feedback and innovation in the Kitchen also led to the replacement of our original grilled menu options, introduced in 1989, with an entirely new chargrilled recipe prepared on a custom-designed grill. For nearly twenty-five years, customers had seen the original grilled sandwich as a healthy option, but not a craveable one like the original Chick-fil-A Chicken Sandwich. Customers gave it good scores but not great scores, and we didn't want anybody to think they had to sacrifice enjoyment at Chick-fil-A for nutrition. So the innovation team went to work in Hatch and the Kitchen.

The menu team started working on a different marinade recipe, but the big challenge was a grilling capability that would mimic a backyard-quality grill. We couldn't do fire. We didn't have gas in the restaurants, and we didn't want to go down that road. It had to be electric, but we had to figure out a way to mimic the grill marks and the smoked flavor of backyard grilling.

Our engineers, who were part of the food development group in marketing led by Roger Shealy, were looking at the equipment already in the marketplace and talking to those equipment companies about how they might adapt equipment to get the product attributes we wanted. We weren't getting the flavor and texture we wanted; the existing equipment options were cooking too much of the moisture out of the chicken or the grill marks weren't what we wanted. They concluded that nothing on the market could deliver the end result we were seeking, so we had to select a company to work with us to design, engineer, and build a custom piece of equipment. Garland Grills designed a grill with cast-iron grates that grilled ten fillets with just the right amount of pressure to sear in the flavor and the moisture, top and bottom.

Keeping the brand relevant through innovation also meant never losing the connection of the future with the past. For example, fresh design elements in many restaurants include a large table made from reclaimed wood for community seating. And over the table hangs a chandelier made by an Atlanta artist using Coca-Cola bottles that have been heated and flattened. Both the table and the chandelier connect to Truett, who set up a front-yard stand to sell Cokes in the 1920s when he was eight years old, and who also had a heart for folks needing a second chance. The tables are made by men working through "A Better Way Ministries" to deal with life-controlling issues such as drug and alcohol addictions.

Innovating Through Organizational Flexibility

We didn't limit innovation to Hatch, the Kitchen, or the marketing department. In fact, we encouraged everyone throughout the organization, at the home office and in restaurants, to share their ideas. We promoted innovative thinking by encouraging people to move around in the Chick-fil-A organization. The company had an organization chart, but a significant people-development policy evolved that allowed flexibility and opportunities to work in different positions within the company.

Nobody got pigeonholed for a career. A field marketing rep or an IT professional or an advertising expert could do something else. Great thinkers continued to learn and seek new challenges and add value to everything they touched. They were rewarded financially and with fresh, challenging assignments, and they grew.

The company grew as well. We created business generalists who then moved up through the organization and were better able to grasp the totality of the business. They could work on capacity or investment or marketing or store growth, and in a later context, help make better decisions.

As part of this commitment to developing talent outside the scope of their current responsibilities, each executive committee member had a formal mentor relationship with at least two people per year from outside their department. They made business trips together and spent time together regularly over lunch, asking and answering questions in a completely transparent, completely confidential manner. The relationship allowed each to understand the other's job and perspective on work.

As the staff grew in size, we expanded the program to other officer levels. It was not unusual for people to have outside coaches, but the best executive coach was often somebody already in the organization who was outside their department. The cross-departmental relationships illuminated the brand touchpoints circle from new points of view and triggered innovation.

ELEVEN

The Cows Go to the College Football Championship

By 2005, we had renewed our three-year contract two times for the Chick-fil-A Peach Bowl. Regionally, the bowl had succeeded, selling out year after year. Participants and fans were telling us and the bowl staff that the game was unlike any other bowl experience out there. It wasn't just a game; they enjoyed genuine hospitality while they engaged in a truly fun experience. On the national stage, however, the Chick-fil-A Peach Bowl was not in the top ten bowls, principally defined by team payouts and TV ratings. We all wanted to enhance the game and the entire bowl brand—what it stood for, the fan experience, as well as the experience for teams and the media.

Although corporations were paying millions of dollars for the right to have their names attached to bowl games, the media often ignored the sponsor. The Chick-fil-A Peach Bowl remained the

"Peach Bowl" in many, perhaps most, media references. Nokia at that time sponsored the Sugar Bowl, FedEx the Orange Bowl, Tostitos the Fiesta Bowl, and other companies had the same issue.

Sponsorships provided between 30 and 45 percent of the cash flow for a typical bowl, yet the media seldom gave sponsors credit for what they were contributing to college football's postseason.

For the better part of two years, I was meeting regularly with Gary Stokan and Leeman Bennett, the former Atlanta Falcons head coach who was chairman of the bowl. Each time I was asking, in one way or another, "How can we help you guys take the bowl to the next level so that you are willing to give us the name—a win-win for both of us?"

We had three complementary goals:

- Offer greater team payouts
- With the higher payouts, renegotiate contracts with the conferences to get higher ranked teams
- Better teams would lead to greater audiences and potentially larger network rights fees for the bowl

We believed we could become one of the best, if not the best, non-BCS game, and we wanted to use that success to negotiate with ESPN for an exclusive time slot on New Year's Eve. We had done well with December 31, and we wanted to get it locked in and unopposed—another little Blue Ocean. And we were willing to entertain a higher title sponsor rights fee to make all this happen.

As an added bonus, we (Peach Bowl, Inc., and Chick-fil-A) could use improved performance to also generate more money for charity. And in the back of our minds, we also hoped that if the major conferences ever changed from the BCS format to a four-team playoff championship format, it might help position the Chick-fil-A Peach

Bowl to bid as a host site. After a lot of brainstorming and negotiating, the three of us put a deal together, and Leeman pre-shopped the "Chick-fil-A Bowl" package to the bowl's executive committee.

At a meeting of the executive committee, Bob Coggins (Peach Bowl, Inc., board member and former Delta CMO) said that eight or nine years earlier, he never would have supported changing the name to the Chick-fil-A Bowl. But seeing what Chick-fil-A had meant for the bowl, he supported the change. The Peach Bowl, Inc., board agreed. So the name was changed to the Chick-fil-A Bowl. We were able to accomplish our mutual goals for higher team payout, higher ranked teams, higher TV rights fees, and more charity dollars.

About the same time, Gary Stokan floated the idea of a second, lower-tier bowl game for Atlanta. Gary, Leeman, and I discussed whether the city could handle a second game, whether our volunteer infrastructure would support it, and whether it might be lost in the bowl landscape.

The NCAA had recently announced that schools could add a twelfth game to their schedules, and Leeman asked whether we should consider a game at the beginning of the season, like the former Kickoff Classic in New Jersey in the 1980s and '90s. I loved the idea on the spot, and said if Atlanta had such a game, we would be interested in sponsoring it. Gary liked the kickoff idea, too, and dropped the second bowl possibility to pursue this.

Not long after, Gary and our sponsorship team were in New York working on the marketing calendar with ESPN and the bowl. ESPN's college football program director, Dave Brown, and Gary had been talking with the University of Alabama and Clemson University about the possibility of playing in the first Chick-fil-A Kickoff, and they were working hard for a commitment from Alabama. While we were at ESPN, they were on the phone with Alabama. Dave said we would need to commit more financial resources to get Alabama into the game, and I agreed that Chick-fil-A would help with that. Gary got a two-year commitment from Alabama head coach Nick Saban, and that got the Chick-fil-A Kickoff off the ground. ESPN gave us a great time slot, and Clemson committed to play Alabama in the inaugural game. The next year Alabama played Virginia Tech.

Looking back, Coach Saban was the final piece of the puzzle. As of this writing, Alabama has played in the game five times and won every time.

Shortly after the first Chick-fil-A Kickoff Game, Gary Stokan came to us with another college football opportunity for Atlanta. The National Football Foundation, which operates the College Football Hall of Fame, was considering moving the site out of South Bend, Indiana. Gary thought we could get the Hall of Fame in Atlanta. Steve Hatchell, president of the foundation, said he was interested in Atlanta, so Gary recommended to the Peach Bowl Inc., board of directors that we raise the money to build and operate the Hall of Fame.

After months of discussion, the board chose to do that. Gary asked the board to put up the initial $5 million of seed money to start doing the real work of searching for a site and designing the experience. We established Atlanta Hall Management, Inc., created a separate board of directors, and I was asked to serve as chairman.

When Gary and I asked Truett to match the bowl's $5 million commitment for the project, Truett agreed. He liked the concept and was happy for the opportunity to support his hometown in this way. Not long after that, Frank Poe, president of the Georgia World Congress Center Authority, approached Gary and the board and said he wanted to create a better "front door" to the Georgia World Congress Center than a parking lot. Would we be interested in the Marietta Street parking lot on the east side of the GWCC?

We were! Atlanta Hall Management signed a long-term lease for the property adjacent to the GWCC, across the street from Centennial Olympic Park and an easy walk to the Georgia Dome, Philips Arena, and the future site of the Mercedes-Benz Stadium.

About a year into the project, Gary Stokan stepped down as president of the Hall of Fame to focus full-time on growing the Chick-fil-A Bowl enterprise, and John Stephenson, formerly of Troutman Sanders law firm, was named president.

We intentionally designed the space to be a great guest interaction that would mimic a game-day experience, not a museum, and we had selected the key vendors and other suppliers to build it, but we were still short several million dollars. We were within two weeks of the deadline to meet the line-of-credit contract with the bank, and I was losing sleep. Like all the other sponsors to date, Chick-fil-A had signed a five-year financial commitment. Then, lying in bed one morning, it occurred to me that Chick-fil-A was not just another sponsor. We were highly invested in college football, the bowl, the kickoff games, and the Chick-fil-A Peach Bowl Challenge golf event. Maybe we should be bringing more than money to the table. Maybe we could bring the Chick-fil-A guest experience into the Hall of Fame.

The next night I wrote a proposal for Chick-fil-A to be not the title sponsor but the presenting sponsor, with a thirty-year commitment. Our commitment would be to help Atlanta Hall Management create a guest experience that delivered the unexpected: history, game-day traditions, heroes, wrapped in great hospitality. And a thirty-year marketing partner. I sent the proposal to Dan Cathy, and within forty-eight hours (bless his heart!), he said, "Let's do it." Then, inside of one week, I presented it to the National Football Foundation and the Atlanta Hall Management boards, and they approved it. It was a wonderful demonstration of Dan picking up the mantle from his dad and saying, "I understand college football has been very good for Chick-fil-A, and this will be good for Atlanta." We met the bank covenants, which prompted additional sponsors to join us since they now could see the path for the Hall of Fame to open.

With the advent of touch-screen and radio-activated technology and videos, visitors to the College Football Hall of Fame and Chick-fil-A Fan Experience could walk through the space and find anything they wanted on *any* Hall of Fame member, any institution (more than 725) that plays college football, any bowl game that's ever been played, the history of any championship, anything to do with college football. Division I, Division II, Division III, historically black colleges and universities, all of it. They could also engage with all the traditions fans love, like tailgating, bands, and cheerleaders, and relive great game memories and game calls. It was all in there.

The College Football Hall of Fame and Chick-fil-A Fan Experience now entertains more than 250,000 visitors and two hundred events each year, and there's no reason to think it won't continue to grow.

Since I retired, my successor, Jon Bridges, has elevated Chick-fil-A's marketing commitment to the Hall even further, recognized by the official name being changed to the Chick-fil-A College Football Hall of Fame.

Seeking the Final CFP Bowl Slot

As we were building equity around the Chick-fil-A Bowl and the Chick-fil-A Kickoff Game, the "Power Five" conferences and Notre Dame created the College Football Playoff concept: a four-team playoff with the semifinal games rotating among six bowl cities. They made it clear that they were going to protect the four BCS (Bowl Championship Series) bowls (Rose, Orange, Sugar, Fiesta). Also, Jerry Jones was building a new Cowboys Stadium in Dallas, and because the

Cotton Bowl had a tremendous legacy, Dallas would probably be the fifth site. There was only one CFP bowl site to be determined.

Atlanta was in the mix, along with Orlando, Jacksonville, San Antonio, and San Diego. Atlanta had great assets to offer, with plenty of hotels, the Georgia World Congress Center, the new Atlanta Falcons' stadium that would open in 2017, and the history of an incredible bowl experience that Peach Bowl, Inc., and Chick-fil-A had created together.

The financial relationships between ESPN, the College Football Playoff, and the bowls themselves would be significantly different. The CFP was negotiating a deal with ESPN for the rights to broadcast these seven games, as well as the marketing rights to use all the trademarks and the marketing affiliation with the six bowl games and the National Championship. This aggregate deal of seven games every year was officially the "College Football Playoff."

If Atlanta's bid was selected, Atlanta would be guaranteed one of the top six bowl games every year. Every third year, we would host one of the CFP semifinal games, and the bowl title sponsor would have marketing rights and advertising content in not only the Atlanta game, but all seven CFP games.

At the same time, if the CFP selected the Chick-fil-A Bowl, then the Chick-fil-A Bowl board of directors would give up much of its control of the game (team selection, TV contract, ticket pricing, etc.). Inherently, the bowl would end its exclusive affiliations with the SEC and the ACC.

For Chick-fil-A, if we wanted to remain the bowl's title sponsor, our investment in the game and the entire college football season would likely triple. Let me assure you, it was not an automatic yes at the home office. But by that time, we had invested sixteen years in the bowl, and our expanding presence in college football had yielded significant brand awareness and relationships across the country. If we didn't commit, then one of two things would happen: the CFP would choose Atlanta and another brand would step up and become the title sponsor of the bowl; or Atlanta would not be chosen and our bowl would become just another of the thirty-plus non-CFP post-season games.

The multistep bid process continued over several months in 2012 and 2013.

The CFP would select the six bowls, then negotiate a contract with ESPN. After that, the network would negotiate with sponsors. I went to Truett and explained that if we supported the bowl in its bid with the CFP, we would have to follow up with a multiyear financial commitment to ESPN. But we would enjoy national visibility with this audience at levels we had never experienced. Inherently, it would support our national growth.

Once again, he agreed that college football and its fans had been "very good for Chick-fil-A," and he supported pursuing a commitment.

To make a long story short, the CFP selected Atlanta's bid to become one of the six cities in the rotation, with the stipulation that "Peach" be brought back to the name. Once again, the game would be the Chick-fil-A Peach Bowl. That was not ideal, but not a deal killer for us, because eight years of the "Chick-fil-A Bowl" had established a strong connection between our brand and the game.

The first College Football Playoff would follow the 2014 season, and the Chick-fil-A Peach Bowl would host its first semifinal game following the 2016 season. If any initiative announced that Chick-fil-A had become a national brand, the College Football Playoff was it.

Opening in Manhattan

We were becoming a national brand before we had opened restaurants nationwide. That's the only way to explain opening our first restaurants in a suburb of Portland and Seattle with each having first-day sales of sixty-five thousand dollars. The brand was known, and there was pent-up demand for it. Some of that demand might have been from southeastern transplants, but not all of it.

For years before we opened our first Manhattan store, Kelly Ripa was telling Regis Philbin and later Michael Strahan on their morning TV show how much she loved Chick-fil-A. The first Manhattan store opened on the day after her forty-fifth birthday in October 2015, and she insisted she was going to camp out with the first one hundred customers so she could get free Chick-fil-A for a year. That kind of love helped create demand for Chick-fil-A and also created fun connections.

When the store opened at 1000 Sixth Avenue, AdAge.com announced that Chick-fil-A Operator Oscar Fittipaldi was "the newest celebrity to arrive in New York."[9] The first Manhattan location was a major financial investment, but when it came to introducing Chick-fil-A to not only Manhattan but the world, this location was another crucial step. Also, we were intentionally developing our prototype in-line urban design to take to other cities. There is no greater laboratory than Manhattan to do that!

It turned out there was even more demand than we realized in Manhattan. During the first full year of operation, that store enjoyed more than $10 million in sales. It was a very expensive rent deal and it was expensive to build, but at that volume, Oscar did fine. Like Kelly Ripa, a lot of New Yorkers who had been waiting for us to come were excited when we got there, and they showed up.

As far as brand consciousness, we were on the way to becoming a national brand. Yet there was plenty of opportunity to grow. Coca-Cola once announced, "We're going be ubiquitous." And they did just that. They started in the United States, and then they went from there to the world.

We still have years of opportunity in the USA. If we penetrated just the top one hundred markets in the United States at the same rate we have penetrated Atlanta today, we would have more than eight thousand restaurants. We're a little more than twenty-three hundred restaurants at this writing. Chick-fil-A could be blessed with a long runway of opportunities in this great country.

TWELVE

Life and Legacy

What's the best way to ensure that the next generation of the Chick-fil-A organization has the historical context of the way Truett and the first executive committee made decisions? What value lens was virtually every major decision seen through for more than thirty-five years—decisions about initiatives, investments, and people? What common themes weighed heavily with Truett, which, in turn, he coached and modeled for us?

Other than the corporate purpose, these went unwritten for decades because we implicitly learned and understood them. Then in 2013, a group of executive committee members and other long-term leaders said, "If we don't make a conscious effort to capture in writing how he led us, then the next generation will have to discover it on their own, if that's even possible when the founder is no longer around." We're the ones who have to coach it now. So a group of us did just that—we wrote down the core values that shaped and filtered virtually every vital decision we made during the course of more than thirty years of working with Truett. It took us more than a year to do the work and agree, but here they are. You will see some familiar themes.

Being a Good Steward

As I write about Truett Cathy's stewardship, the things he did are a reflection of who he was. My hope is that the next generation would not simply copy his actions, but embrace his heart so that the actions flow naturally. Truett didn't keep a list of ways to be a good steward. He simply was!

He was modeling stewardship long before "being a faithful steward" became a tenet of the Chick-fil-A corporate purpose. He was a good steward of his relationships, beginning with his family. He and Jeannette were about to celebrate their sixty-seventh wedding anniversary when Truett "graduated." The two of them saw their children as gifts from God to be nurtured and taught, and they kept in mind that their children always belonged to Him.

In the Dwarf House restaurant, which he operated for twenty-one years before the first Chick-fil-A opened, several employees worked there for decades and often spoke of the love and respect they felt for Truett and he for them. One of the oft-told stories centered on Eddie White, a young African American man who worked at the Dwarf House in the early 1950s. Eddie didn't have enough money for college, so the waitresses put a mayonnaise jar on the counter and labeled it "Eddie's College Fund." When school was about to start and the money collected would only cover half the year, Truett wrote a check for the balance. Good stewardship? As an adult, Eddie White worked for three decades in the Clayton County school system developing other children.

In 1973 Truett began offering one thousand dollar college scholarships to restaurant team members. An industry first. By that time he had already been teaching Sunday school to thirteen-year-old boys for more than twenty years. Those boys, he believed, had been entrusted to their parents and also teachers, Scout leaders, and others like himself, and he took his stewardship opportunity seriously.

Truett believed that every dollar that flowed through Chick-fil-A belonged to God, and we were to be stewards of it. That point of view allowed him to be both generous and thrifty. Every dollar mattered, whether invested in the business, people, or charity.

Building Long-Term Relationships

Truett's relationships were for life. He and Jeannette were married for almost sixty-seven years, and ideally, he wanted all his relationships to be as permanent as his marriage. He even used those words, *it's a marriage*, when he was interviewing potential Operators for Chick-fil-A restaurants. He was giving his full commitment, and he wanted the same in return. In his mind, if you were going to be a part of Chick-fil-A, there was no reason for you to ever go anywhere else in your career. I will always remember him saying that to me.

From a purely business point of view, experience comes with time, as does institutional learning, and he didn't want that stuff walking out the door. The inefficiency of turnover and retraining hurts more than just the bottom line. The restaurant and the company do not run as smoothly, and customers notice. At a deeper level, with time people come to understand one another's hearts and motivations and grow into closer alignment.

At the same time, one has to balance long tenure with making sure people don't become lazy, stale, or out of touch. So we spent a lot of time, effort, and money on continuous improvement, training, and education, as well as moving people around to new assignments to keep them sharp.

Providing Hospitality

Truett always insisted on the highest quality ingredients and the best recipes, but he also knew that good food alone would not guarantee success. Hospitality became his major competitive edge in creating a sustainable business at the Dwarf House.

It's interesting that it took us almost thirty years as a brand to figure out how to translate Truett's heart for hospitality into the Chick-fil-A business. It took him asking us to say, "My pleasure," and that phrase became emblematic of his heart of hospitality. Once we understood, hospitality became a powerful engine for the brand.

"My pleasure" creates an immediate communication that you really do matter. When said, it almost invariably gets a smile back from the customer. So why did Truett do it? He had the gift of hospitality, and he couldn't help himself. But the bigger reality became clear—the phrase is transformative in terms of the guest's experience.

Hospitality is not natural for the fast-food category, and quite frankly, at a personal level, not everybody has the gift of hospitality. So when we talked about the hospitality director at a Chick-fil-A restaurant, we learned that Operators had to be able to spot the gift of hospitality. Because one of the great things about people with the gift of hospitality is they attract more people with the same gift.

Taking Personal Responsibility

Personal accountability is empowering. And it was an important aspect of Truett's relationships. When he selected people to work at Chick-fil-A or to become restaurant Operators, he sought people he knew could do the job, and then he trusted them to do it. He gave us the keys then stepped out of the way. Sometimes he literally said, "I trust your judgment." But even when he didn't say the words, we knew he did. I knew he did.

That trust gave us the feeling, and that sense of responsibility, that we were acting on his behalf—and long before WWJD ("What Would Jesus Do?") bracelets were created, we approached every major decision asking ourselves, "What would Truett do?"

We were personally accountable to him, to the brand, and to our customers. We were accountable in the deals we created, in the relationships we built in the business, in our behavior on the road, in how we talked about the business, even in our language on the golf course. When he placed his trust in us, we responded with personal accountability.

He never followed me around to be my personal accountability judge. It was up to me to know why I existed, what I stood for, and what the business stood for. I was accountable.

I told people at Chick-fil-A not to worry about losing their jobs. Not to worry about messing up. As a part of Chick-fil-A, they were implicitly entrusted to make their own judgments. They would learn. They would do the right thing. That is empowering.

Choosing Personal Influence over Position Power

Chick-fil-A has a history of not giving anyone a title until their performance already looks like that role for a long time. For example, Jimmy Collins was executive vice president well into the 1980s, even though he was doing all the work and taking all the responsibility of a corporate president. When Truett announced at an Operator seminar that Jimmy Collins was now the president of Chick-fil-A and everybody stood up and applauded him and roared, most everybody was either thinking or saying to the person next to them, "Well that's certainly overdue."

Truett and Jimmy were not concerned about the title. I've heard them both say many times, "If I ever have to use position power to influence somebody, I'm probably only going to get to do that once. And if I have to do it at all, it probably does not bode well for their future." So they sought people who could perform in the strength of their personality and their values, not because of their position.

They were looking for people who could create followership and get things done completely independent of what their title was. If their influence and their performance depended on a title, they were the wrong person for Chick-fil-A. We've hired many people in our business at a title level significantly below one they had somewhere else. The ability to inspire teamwork and rally people around a mission or project are much more important than position power.

Even at the highest level, Truett almost never used the power of his position to force the company in a direction that the executive committee disagreed with. As sole owner, he could have, but he seldom did.

Having Fun

Truett never took himself too seriously. On Cow Appreciation Day, Truett wore his favorite Cow attire—not an entire Cow costume, but enough to make people smile. He loved walking through an airport with a bag filled with plush Cows so he could give them away and make people laugh. He was sneaky funny, with a dry wit that would catch you off guard and make you wonder, *Where did that come from?*

One of the virtues that evolved in the business was a tangible effort to be unexpectedly fun. For us, it's more fun to work in an environment like that, but the primary reason was because Truett was unexpectedly fun.

These six legacy principles have served CFA well. They are truly cultural pillars that have helped keep CFA's leaders and "family" focused on what makes CFA uniquely different.

Afterword

At the Rose Bowl, Remembering Truett

January 1, 2015. It was two years after Truett and I stood on the sidelines together for the last time at the Chick-fil-A Peach Bowl. I was two thousand miles—and a whole world—away, standing on the sidelines inside the Rose Bowl in Pasadena, California. It was the first semifinal of the new College Football Playoff, and Chick-fil-A was a sponsor.

It was also the first day of my last year at Chick-fil-A. I would turn sixty-five in May and, thus, would retire, but I was scheduled to serve the entire year as a coach to my chief marketing officer successor, Jon Bridges, and as a mentor to other staff. Jon and his wife, Amy, were with Dianne and me, and we had just finished touring an amazing fan engagement production outside the Rose Bowl, orchestrated by members of our marketing staff, with the help of local Operators and their team members. Their activation of Chick-fil-A food, the Cows, and fan activities rivaled anything produced by larger, traditional brands in the college football space, including ESPN, AT&T, Coca-Cola, and Kia.

In that historic and magnificent venue on an absolutely perfect day, I saw two prominent Chick-fil-A logos. And there was a Chick-fil-A free offer at each seat. We would later learn that more than 30 million homes watched the game, and more than 150 million viewers would watch all seven College Football Playoff games that year. Chick-fil-A would have multiple Cow TV spots in all these games, along with in-game features. Chick-fil-A had become a national brand.

I thought of Truett, my friend and mentor. He had passed away a few months earlier, on September 8, 2014. He would have relished this moment.

I considered Truett's positive influence on others by simply demonstrating how to live an effective Christian life in the context of building a business and a brand. He never preached a sermon other than the life he lived. He loved God, he loved his family, and he loved his neighbor. Out of that love grew a culture that allowed Chick-fil-A—and me personally—to thrive. To experience a professional and personal journey beyond my dreams—from a simple sandwich to a great fast-food restaurant, to a unique caring and hospitality experience, to *a brand many people cannot see themselves living without.*

Thank you, Truett. Thank you, Lord.

Acknowledgments

My forty-three-year career has flown by. Writing *Covert Cows and Chick-fil-A* has led me to take a deliberate look back, and I have been amazed at the privilege and blessings I have experienced. I could never have dreamed of such a career when I chose a marketing major at Auburn. And yet, I have also concluded that many of the key lessons and principles I learned during the course of my career are *not* unique to me. They are available to any business and brand leader.

The American free enterprise system is still alive and well, providing fertile ground for entrepreneurs. Two significant entrepreneurs impacted my life, my dad and Truett Cathy. Then there were the thousands of Chick-fil-A Operators who mirrored Truett's entrepreneurial spirit. Our US culture needs to hear, understand, and appreciate the incredible blessing we have of being in an economic environment that catapults men and women like them. There is no more dramatic and illustrative entrepreneurial story than that of Chick-fil-A.

And, as I have written, the greatest influence on building a successful business and brand is its culture, which rises and falls on leadership. Truett understood the role of culture, and he made it a top priority and personal focus. He was intentional about surrounding himself with men and women who were similarly committed.

When I made the decision to pursue a marketing degree at Auburn University, I dreamed of one day working and growing in such a culture—having a fun and challenging job in Atlanta, Georgia. Never did I dream of the career, friendships, and incredible experiences God would allow me to be a part of. And none was more unbelievable than working for a man like Truett Cathy and his aspiring company as their chief marketing executive: building a team and strategy from scratch, and seeing it blossom into a brand infrastructure to support some of the finest entrepreneurs in America, Chick-fil-A Operators. I unabashedly thank God and Truett.

I praise God for all the men and women before and during my Chick-fil-A years. At the top of the list, Dianne, an amazing wife, lover, mother, and counselor. She and our children, Joy and Josh, were unwavering in their commitment and support for me in good and in challenging times. And as you may have noticed, she often gave me sound and godly counsel.

And then all the others I have mentioned. Men and women whom God used in unique and often underappreciated ways to help guide or sharpen me, and in the process bless my career, family, and ultimately, Chick-fil-A. Their names are in here for a reason.

On a different note, I want to be clear for any member of the greater Chick-fil-A family reading this. As Jimmy Collins reminded us upon his retirement as president in 2001: success is often harder to sustain than to create. I hope my story, and the portion of the Chick-fil-A story that I experienced, will help you understand what was negotiable and nonnegotiable in the Chick-fil-A culture, starting with the Corporate Purpose. It's up to you to make those judgments for the future along with your Chick-fil-A peers. May God help you to choose wisely what the cornerstones of Chick-fil-A's culture will be.

And for those readers not a part of Chick-fil-A, I am honored you took your valuable time to read my attempt at scribing my story. I hope you have found some nuggets on the role of culture in building a great business or brand, and maybe a few strategic ideas that might challenge some of your current marketing and brand-building paradigms.

Personally, I would love to see more consumer-facing companies learn how to grow their businesses and brands through genuine, personal engagement with customers. Maybe this book could help someone start that journey!

My journey and my story were not written alone. They were written under the strong influence of God, His Son, and Holy Spirit; my sweet wife, Dianne, and later, my children, Joy and Josh; Truett Cathy and his family; Jimmy Collins, Chick-fil-A's first chief operating officer and president; Chick-fil-A's executive committee for more than thirty years; a wonderful and wise marketing leadership team; hundreds of Operators who gave me great feedback and support; millions of customers talking to us and me through a myriad of channels. In all, I marvel at the amazing story God graciously allowed me to be a part of—one that ultimately blesses millions of customers every day.

I could not have turned that story into this book without the help of Dick Parker, my partner in writing and wise counsel. Dick has helped cowrite or ghostwrite many books, but none better qualified him to work with me than his helping Truett Cathy write his four books.

Jenny Baumgartner, chief editor for this book at Thomas Nelson, has been a huge help with her counsel, editing suggestions, and activating the tremendous team at Thomas Nelson, HarperCollins. As a first-time author, I could not have done this (or enjoyed it!) without their help.

Jonathan Merkh, my literary agent, has an extensive résumé in publishing, and he has done a superb job helping navigate me through the world of publishers and how to work with them. I could not have gotten this project off the ground without his help!

Life is fast. As I have reflected on the story that God put me in the middle of, I am reminded that it has gone by quickly. Under His leadership and favor, it has been rich in meaningful relationships, fun, and experiences (good and challenging). I am incredibly grateful for His putting me in a company with a clear purpose, and because of that association, helping me to discover and enjoy my purpose as well.

May you always know your purpose.

—Steve

> Teach us to number our days,
> that we may gain a heart of wisdom. . . .
> May the favor of the Lord our God rest on us;
> establish the work of our hands for us—
> yes, establish the work of our hands.
>
> —Psalm 90:12, 17 NIV

Appendix

Influencers

So many people have influenced me in my life and career. Following are just a few:

Dianne and our kids. Dianne has been an amazing life partner, counselor, and mother. She was fully engaged in my career, and still is. Our children always supported my work and must have enjoyed what they saw—they both have marketing careers. Joy and Josh have become passionate followers of Christ and are terrific parents with their mates Dan Roark and Susan Breeding Robinson, respectively. We are having a ball watching our four grandchildren bloom and mature: Kyla, Meira, Amos, and Price.

John B. Robinson, my father, was a man who coached me about everything. He took nothing for granted. As a small-business man, he lived out the challenges and rewards of running a business while serving others with integrity. And my mom, Martha Robinson, was always an encourager and champion for me.

Truett Cathy was second only to my dad and maybe the most

influential man in my life. The story in this book speaks for itself—God used Truett to impact me immensely.

Jerry Batts, Auburn fraternity brother who introduced me to Dianne, and still a great friend today. Without Jerry, I may never have met the most important person and friend in my life.

George Horton, dean at Auburn University's College of Business in 1972. George's encouragement and counsel to me was life changing.

Vernon Fryberger, dean at Northwestern's Medill School of Journalism and Advertising. Dr. Fryberger's willingness to bend the rules to accept my late entry into the graduate program at Medill was an act of grace that transformed my marketing perspectives and career opportunities.

Frank Walters, my supervisor at Texas Instruments, was patient with me and gave me enough rope to experiment and learn, particularly in the world of direct-response marketing.

Dan Howells at Six Flags Over Texas gave me a shot at the Seven Seas assignment and patiently tutored me. His brother, Bob Howells, was a Northwestern classmate and friend. I became a part of the Six Flags organization for seven years because of Dan.

George Delanoy, vice president of marketing for Six Flags, Inc., was a strong mentor on strategic planning and brand.

Jim Pemberton, sales and promotions manager at Six Flags Over Texas, was a great tutor and a wonderful friend and marketing partner.

Spurgeon Richardson, director of marketing and later general manager at Six Flags Over Georgia, was a great mentor and friend. Spurge gave me a shot when I was just twenty-seven to be part of his marketing leadership team, and later, to serve as marketing director for the park.

Jimmy Collins, my direct supervisor at Chick-fil-A until his retirement in 2001. Jimmy and Truett were two of the finest men and leaders I have *ever* met and worked with. They shaped and led the cultural underpinnings (which I have unpacked) that equipped and empowered me to have the thirty-four-year run I had with Chick-fil-A.

Dr. Ken Bernhardt, Regents Professor of Marketing Emeritus, Georgia State University, one of my best friends in the Atlanta business community and an amazing mentor on research and customer listening.

David Salyers, my first marketing professional hire at Chick-fil-A, was always part of my department leadership team in multiple roles. David is a tremendous developer of talent and teamwork and a trustworthy friend.

Sandy Causey, my executive assistant for virtually my entire Chick-fil-A career, served others constantly, usually without request. Nobody understood and lived the Chick-fil-A culture of love, respect, trust, and grace better than Sandy. She anticipated needs and sought to fulfill them. An encourager, she brought a spirit of gentleness, affirmation, and hospitality with her every day. She loved others, beginning with her husband, Bo, and their family, and expressed that love with simple acts of kindness. And using her gift of hospitality, she organized major Chick-fil-A events around the bowl and kickoff games. She found ways to make large events feel more personal, so that even as Chick-fil-A grew larger, it continued to feel like a small, family company. She got the details right so I didn't have to worry about them.

Don Perry was the first public relations officer I hired at Chick-fil-A and was a great friend to both Truett Cathy and me. Don led the search and selection of Chick-fil-A's first public relations firm, Cohn & Wolfe. He graduated to glory in the summer of 2012.

Bob Cohn, principal in Cohn & Wolfe, the first public relations firm Don Perry and I hired for Chick-fil-A. Bob brought proactive energy to media outreach and grand openings. He helped us in early grand openings on the ground activation and events. Bob is still a great friend today. In 2018 C&W merged with Burson-Marsteller to create one of the world's largest communications companies.

Glen Jackson and his team and Jackson Spalding also played a major role on our media relations and nonpaid communications. They contributed greatly to supporting Truett as the primary spokesman for the brand, product rollouts, grand openings, crisis management, and CFA-sponsored partnerships.

Dr. Bill Baran ("Biscuit Bill") was the first food research and development officer for Chick-fil-A.

Woody Faulk played a crucial role in our department, serving on our marketing leadership team while holding multiple roles of leadership around menu development, store design, hospitality innovation, and the evolution of our innovation process. Woody also blessed our family in a unique way: he was one of the founders and board president for the creation and operation of Heritage Prep School, which has been foundational in the education of Josh's three children.

David Farmer was a key member of our marketing leadership team and driver of perfecting the innovation process, first around food and then the entire business. David led the effort to design, build, and staff Hatch and the Kitchen innovation centers. I knew David for several years before I joined Chick-fil-A; I've watched him mature into a tremendous leader.

Jack Sentell and Barry White were pioneers of field marketing and Chick-fil-A's licensing concept. They were important members of my leadership team, men whose counsel I trusted and always valued.

Carrie Kurlander was Don Perry's successor and has been part of the marketing leadership team since late 2012. Carrie is a true professional with a great background in politics and at Southern Company.

Stan Richards, founder and CEO of the Richards Group. Great friend and immeasurable contributor to the CFA brand and my life for twenty years.

Brad Todd at the Richards Group. Principal who helped land CFA at TRG. Great brand management perspective from Frito-Lay. A trusted counselor and friend.

Jon Bridges was part of the marketing leadership team for my last six years at Chick-fil-A, and before that he was chief information officer for the company. He brought a customer-facing digital focus to our leadership team. Jon succeeded me as chief marketing officer. Formerly with Accenture, Jon is both strategic and analytical.

Pastors Bill Sutton, Clark Hutchinson, Mark Henry, Crawford Loritts, and Gary Hewins. Amazing men of the Word and counsel. Every one of them have spoken biblical truth that shaped and changed my life, marriage, and family. I'm blessed to count them all as friends.

Dennis Rainey, founder and just-retired CEO of FamilyLife, subsidiary of Cru. One of the finest leaders I have ever known. He could have been a leader anywhere, but the Lord called him and Barbara to a life of equipping marriages and families. Honored to serve on his board for more than twenty years.

The Coombes family in Christchurch, New Zealand, who took me in as an exchange student and helped me see the world from a new perspective.

Gary Stokan, president of Peach Bowl, Inc., joined us on an amazing nineteen-year journey of growth and innovation that led to multiple Chick-fil-A Peach Bowl affiliations: the bowl, the kickoff game, the Challenge golf tournament, the Hall of Fame initiative, and Chick-fil-A's role as a College Playoff sponsor. Along the way, we developed dozens of meaningful friendships with his staff, conference commissioners, athletic directors, and coaches, including Peach Bowl staff members David Epps, Derek Martin, Matt Garvey, Anton

Dawson, Chris Hughes, Dan West, Benji Hollis, and their administrator Patty Young (who really ran things).

Zac Grant and Charlie and Chris Busbee were tremendous ambassadors for us to build the relationships and support for Chick-fil-A sponsored events, principally the LPGA golf tournament and CFA Peach Bowl Golf Challenge. Their twenty-plus year dedication to this crucial role helped to generate millions in charity donations.

Rob Temple, Burke Magnus, and John Skipper at ESPN . . . without their help and internal support for Chick-fil-A, we would never have become a College Football Playoff partner and sponsor. They are great friends.

Roman Korab, my friend and partner who helped craft our relationship with CBS.

Steve Hatchell, Archie Manning, and Murry Bowden with the National Football Foundation. Without their help and support, the College Football Hall of Fame would never have been moved and opened in Atlanta, not to mention Chick-fil-A's role in it.

Chette Williams, FCA chaplain for Auburn football, was our first personal and financial engagement with FCA. That relationship led to Atlanta and national engagement with FCA, and my son-in-law being part of the Atlanta field team.

Shane Williamson, area director for the Atlanta FCA region when we became engaged with FCA. He is now international CEO for FCA. He remains a great friend and counselor.

Executive committee team members. For thirty-five years, these folks were sharpening iron in not only the business, but in my life. Truett, Dan and Bubba Cathy, Buck McCabe, Jimmy Collins, Perry Ragsdale, Bureon Ledbetter, and Tim Tassapoulos.

My entire marketing team at Chick-fil-A. I have never met a more dedicated, quality group of people in my life. I always trusted them to rise to any challenge and do it with integrity and class.

Chick-fil-A Operators are amazing entrepreneurs who are sold out to continuous improvement, personal quality performance, and influence consistent with Chick-fil-A's purpose. I was motivated to serve them well because I knew they would always do what was best for customers and the reputation of Chick-fil-A.

Notes

1. Ken Blanchard originally coined this term. He granted permission to Chick-fil-A to use the Raving Fan banner.
2. Truett Cathy, *Eat Mor Chikin: Inspire More People: Doing Business the Chick-fil-A Way* (Decatur, GA: Looking Glass Books, 2002), 70.
3. Jimmy Collins, March 28, 2018.
4. Charles R. Swindoll, *Paul: A Man of Grace and Grit* (Nashville: Thomas Nelson, 2002).
5. Cheryl Hall, "Retired State Fair CEO's Thrill Ride Gives New Meaning to Adrenalin Rush," *Dallas News*, September 2015, https://www.dallasnews.com/business/business/2015/09/25/retired-state-fair-ceo-s-thrill-ride-gives-new-meaning-to-adrenalin-rush.
6. *Atlanta Journal-Constitution*, March 20, 1986.
7. "Ad Age Advertising Century: Top 10 Icons," *Ad Age*, March 29, 1999, https://adage.com/article/special-report-the-advertising-century/ad-age-advertising-century-top-10-icons/140157/.
8. Sally Hawkins and Kelly McCarthy, "Jet ski–riding heroes reunite with Houston grandparents they rescued from flood zone," *ABC News*, August 30, 2017, https://abcnews.go.com/US/jet-ski-riding-heroes-rescue-houston-grandparents-flood/story?id=49504683.

9. Adrianne Pasquarelli, "Meet Oscar Fittipaldi, the Owner of NYC's First Full-Service Chick-fil-A," *Ad Age*, August 10, 2015, https://adage.com/article/cmo-strategy/meet-oscar-fittipaldi-owner-manhattan-s-full-service-chick-fil-a/299902/.

About the Author

Steve Robinson is the former executive vice president and chief marketing officer of Chick-fil-A, Inc., 1981–2015. He now serves as a consultant and speaker on organizational culture and brand and marketing architecture. A native of Foley, Alabama, Steve is the son of a farmer and entrepreneur. He holds an associate degree in business administration from Faulkner State Junior College, a bachelor of science in marketing from Auburn University, and a master's in advertising from Medill School of Journalism at Northwestern University. Steve and his wife, Dianne, live in Atlanta. They have two children and four grandchildren.